# Home Networking:
# A Visual Do-It-Yourself Guide

**Brian Underdahl**

**Cisco Press**
800 East 96th Street
Indianapolis, Indiana 46240 USA

# Home Networking: A Visual Do-It-Yourself Guide

Brian Underdahl

Copyright© 2005 Cisco Systems, Inc.

Published by:
Cisco Press
800 East 96th Street
Indianapolis, IN 46240 USA

All rights reserved. No part of this book may be reproduced or transmitted in any form or by any means, electronic or mechanical, including photocopying, recording, or by any information storage and retrieval system, without written permission from the publisher, except for the inclusion of brief quotations in a review.

Printed in the United States of America   2 3 4 5 6 7 8 9 0

Second Printing   November 2004

Library of Congress Cataloging-in-Publication Number: 2004104821

ISBN: 1-58720-127-5

## Warning and Disclaimer

This book is designed to provide information about creating your own home network. Every effort has been made to make this book as complete and as accurate as possible, but no warranty or fitness is implied.

The information is provided on an "as is" basis. The authors, Cisco Press, and Cisco Systems, Inc. shall have neither liability nor responsibility to any person or entity with respect to any loss or damages arising from the information contained in this book or from the use of the discs or programs that may accompany it.

The opinions expressed in this book belong to the author and are not necessarily those of Cisco Systems, Inc. All images of Linksys hardware are provided courtesy of Linksys.

**Publisher**
John Wait

**Editor-in-Chief**
John Kane

**Executive Editor**
Jim Schachterle

**Cisco Representative**
Anthony Wolfenden

**Cisco Press Program Manager**
Nannette M. Noble

**Production Manager**
Patrick Kanouse

**Senior Development Editor**
Christopher Cleveland

**Senior Project Editor**
San Dee Phillips

**Copy Editor**
Katherin Bidwell

**Technical Editors**
Henry Benjamin,
Glenn Fleishman,
Bradley Mitchell

**Editorial Assistant**
Tammi Barnett

**Cover Designer**
Louisa Adair

**Interior Design and Composition**
Mark Shirar

**Indexer**
Brad Herriman

**Proofreader**
Karen Gill

# Feedback Information

At Cisco Press, our goal is to create in-depth technical books of the highest quality and value. Each book is crafted with care and precision, undergoing rigorous development that involves the unique expertise of members from the professional technical community.

Readers' feedback is a natural continuation of this process. If you have any comments regarding how we could improve the quality of this book, or otherwise alter it to better suit your needs, you can contact us through email at feedback@ciscopress.com. Please make sure to include the book title and ISBN in your message.

We greatly appreciate your assistance.

# Trademark Acknowledgments

All terms mentioned in this book that are known to be trademarks or service marks have been appropriately capitalized. Cisco Press or Cisco Systems, Inc. cannot attest to the accuracy of this information. Use of a term in this book should not be regarded as affecting the validity of any trademark or service mark.

# Corporate and Government Sales

Cisco Press offers excellent discounts on this book when ordered in quantity for bulk purchases or special sales.

For more information please contact: U.S. Corporate and Government Sales 1-800-382-3419 corpsales@pearsontechgroup.com

For sales outside the U.S. please contact: International Sales  international@pearsoned.com

CISCO SYSTEMS

**Corporate Headquarters**
Cisco Systems, Inc.
170 West Tasman Drive
San Jose, CA 95134-1706
USA
www.cisco.com
Tel: 408 526-4000
    800 553-NETS (6387)
Fax: 408 526-4100

**European Headquarters**
Cisco Systems International BV
Haarlerbergpark
Haarlerbergweg 13-19
1101 CH Amsterdam
The Netherlands
www-europe.cisco.com
Tel: 31 0 20 357 1000
Fax: 31 0 20 357 1100

**Americas Headquarters**
Cisco Systems, Inc.
170 West Tasman Drive
San Jose, CA 95134-1706
USA
www.cisco.com
Tel: 408 526-7660
Fax: 408 527-0883

**Asia Pacific Headquarters**
Cisco Systems, Inc.
Capital Tower
168 Robinson Road
#22-01 to #29-01
Singapore 068912
www.cisco.com
Tel: +65 6317 7777
Fax: +65 6317 7799

Cisco Systems has more than 200 offices in the following countries and regions. Addresses, phone numbers, and fax numbers are listed on the
**Cisco.com Web site at www.cisco.com/go/offices.**

Argentina • Australia • Austria • Belgium • Brazil • Bulgaria • Canada • Chile • China PRC • Colombia • Costa Rica • Croatia • Czech Republic
Denmark • Dubai, UAE • Finland • France • Germany • Greece • Hong Kong SAR • Hungary • India • Indonesia • Ireland • Israel • Italy
Japan • Korea • Luxembourg • Malaysia • Mexico • The Netherlands • New Zealand • Norway • Peru • Philippines • Poland • Portugal
Puerto Rico • Romania • Russia • Saudi Arabia • Scotland • Singapore • Slovakia • Slovenia • South Africa • Spain • Sweden
Switzerland • Taiwan • Thailand • Turkey • Ukraine • United Kingdom • United States • Venezuela • Vietnam • Zimbabwe

Copyright © 2003 Cisco Systems, Inc. All rights reserved. CCIP, CCSP, the Cisco Arrow logo, the Cisco Powered Network mark, the Cisco Systems Verified logo, Cisco Unity, Follow Me Browsing, FormShare, iQ Net Readiness Scorecard, Networking Academy, and ScriptShare are trademarks of Cisco Systems, Inc.; Changing the Way We Work, Live, Play, and Learn, The Fastest Way to Increase Your Internet Quotient, and iQuick Study are service marks of Cisco Systems, Inc.; and Aironet, ASIST, BPX, Catalyst, CCDA, CCDP, CCIE, CCNA, CCNP, Cisco, the Cisco Certified Internetwork Expert logo, Cisco IOS, the Cisco IOS logo, Cisco Press, Cisco Systems, Cisco Systems Capital, the Cisco Systems logo, Empowering the Internet Generation, Enterprise/Solver, EtherChannel, EtherSwitch, Fast Step, GigaStack, Internet Quotient, IOS, IP/TV, iQ Expertise, the iQ logo, LightStream, MGX, MICA, the Networkers logo, Network Registrar, Packet, PIX, Post-Routing, Pre-Routing, RateMUX, Registrar, SlideCast, SMARTnet, StrataView Plus, Stratm, SwitchProbe, TeleRouter, TransPath, and VCO are registered trademarks of Cisco Systems, Inc. and/or its affiliates in the U.S. and certain other countries.

All other trademarks mentioned in this document or Web site are the property of their respective owners. The use of the word partner does not imply a partnership relationship between Cisco and any other company. (0303R)

Printed in the USA

# About the Author

**Brian Underdahl** is the well-known author of nearly 70 books on a variety of personal computing-related topics. He has been involved with PCs from their beginning, has taught computer classes in several venues, and has been a featured guest on numerous TV shows. He frequently provides technical assistance to businesses.

# About the Technical Reviewers

**Henry Benjamin**, CCIE No. 4695, holds three CCIE certifications (Routing and Switching, ISP Dial, and Communications and Services). He has more than 10 years of experience with Cisco networks and recently worked for Cisco in the internal IT department helping to design and implement networks throughout Australia and Asia.

**Glenn Fleishman** is a technology journalist who contributes regularly to *The Seattle Times*, *The New York Times*, *Macworld* magazine, and *InfoWorld* magazine. He is the coauthor of *The Wireless Networking Starter Kit* and writes about Wi-Fi daily on the web at http://www.wifinetnews.com.

**Bradley Mitchell** is the wireless/networking site writer/editor at http://www.About.com. At About, he has produced online tutorials and reference content on computer networking topics for five years. Bradley is also a senior software engineer at Intel Corporation. During the past 10 years, he has developed, validated, and administered a wide range of network hardware and software systems at Intel with three patents pending. Bradley obtained his master's degree in computer science from the University of Illinois and his bachelor's degree from M.I.T.

# Acknowledgments

I'd like to thank Jim Schachterle for having the vision to suggest this book. He is a true friend.

Thanks also to Fred Holabird, Dennis Gebhardt, and Dave Fitch for taking the time to give their perspective and making sure that this book meets the needs of the readers.

Tammi Barnett, Christopher Cleveland, and Raina Han are just a few of the wonderful Cisco Press team who made things go so smoothly—thank you.

I'd also like to thank the technical review team of Henry Benjamin, Glenn Fleishman, and Bradley Mitchell, who provided some great suggestions for improving the book on the technical front.

This list is way too short, if for no better reason than my inability to know the names of everyone who has contributed to getting this book published.

# Contents at a Glance

# Contents

# Introduction

A home network opens up all sorts of possibilities in the way your family can use its PCs and in the options for entertainment. But choosing the right equipment and creating your own home network can seem like a daunting task. There are so many different options and so much confusing information that the ordinary person can quickly become overwhelmed. You need some straight answers and accurate advice, but you don't want to make networking your hobby. What you want is a simple do-it-yourself guide that enables you to make the right choices, quickly set up your home network, and start having some fun.

This book provides the answers you need by showing you how to choose the best type of network for your home, the equipment you need to buy so that you don't have to make a bunch of trips back to the computer store, and how to get everything working together in the least amount of time.

Even the best experts sometimes run into difficulties and need a little extra help in figuring out what went wrong and how to fix it. That's why most of the chapters conclude with a "What Went Wrong: Your Quick Fix Reference" section to help you troubleshoot some common problems you might encounter and show you how to fix those problems on your own. You might want to think of these troubleshooting sections as the expert looking over your shoulder and helping you through any rough spots.

## Who Should Read This Book

This book is for anyone who wants to make the right choices in setting up a home network as quickly and easily as possible. This book is not loaded with a bunch of computer jargon, and it's not going to take a lot of your time to read this book, either. If you want to become a network engineer, look elsewhere. But if you simply want answers that you can depend on and information you can understand, this is the only home networking book you need.

## How This Book Is Organized

This book follows a logical path that begins by giving you a quick introduction to the reasons why you'll want your own home network and continues by showing you what you need to know to choose the right equipment. You'll find illustrations that explain how things work, pictures that show what the equipment looks like, and images that show what to expect to see on your computer screen.

The book consists of nine chapters in three parts:

- **Part I: Introducing Networking**—This part of the book contains two chapters that introduce you to the absolute basics of home networking:

  **Chapter 1: Why You Want Your Own Network**—In this chapter, you learn about the possibilities that a home network opens up for you and your family.

  **Chapter 2: Home Networking Basics**—See the different types of home networks and get a basic introduction to the pieces that make up a network.

- **Part II: Starting Your Network**—This part provides the real meat of creating your home network. In four chapters, you learn how to choose, install, and configure your home network:

  **Chapter 3: Choosing the Best Network Type**—Before you can begin shopping, it's important to know your home networking options. This chapter shows you how to choose the type of network that's best for your home.

  **Chapter 4: Selecting Network Hardware: Your Complete Buying Guide**—Buying the wrong equipment can cost you a lot of time and money. This chapter tells you how to choose the right equipment the first time.

  **Chapter 5: Installing Your Network Hardware: This Won't Hurt a Bit**—If you aren't a computer expert, the mere thought of installing a bunch of hardware can be a bit stressful. In this chapter, you learn that the process is actually quite easy when you have the right directions.

  **Chapter 6: Configuring Your Network: Bringing Everything Together**—Creating a working home network requires a bit more than physically installing the equipment. This chapter shows you how to set up the software that makes the network work.

- **Part III: Enhancing Your Network**—This final part shows you how to protect your home network from outside threats, how to share parts of the network with your family, and how to make entertainment a part of the network:

  **Chapter 7: Making Your Network Secure: Locking the Network's Door**—You need to protect your family's privacy and safety. In this chapter, you learn how to take some important steps to keep your network your own.

  **Chapter 8: Sharing Your Network**—A network requires some sharing to be useful. This chapter shows you how to share the things that you really want to share on your home network.

  **Chapter 9: The Magic of Entertainment Options**—This final chapter introduces you to some ways to get even more fun out of your home network and how to make your network a part of your family's entertainment.

# Part I   Introducing Networking

This part of the book contains two chapters that introduce you to the absolute basics of home networking.

# Things You'll Learn

- What networks are and how they work

- How a network can help you save money and reduce equipment clutter through sharing

- What types of entertainment a home network can provide

- How home networks can give you more time away from the office

# Chapter 1

# Why You Want
# Your Own Network

If you feel intimidated by the mere idea of trying to understand home networks, don't worry. In this chapter, you'll see that home networks are actually pretty simple to comprehend, are a useful addition to your home, and offer some interesting entertainment options for the whole family. By the end of this chapter, you will understand exactly why a network is something that you really do want for your home.

## Big and Scary Networks: The Simplest Introduction You'll Ever Read

It's easy to be overwhelmed by technical jargon, and the subject of networks has certainly been one of the worst examples of this. It often seems as though the experts like to throw around a lot of complicated language for no better reason than to confuse the uninitiated. Maybe that makes the experts feel as though they know something that's their little secret, but it's not very helpful to people who simply want something that works. Phrases like "Wi-Fi infrastructure mode," "stateful packet inspection," and "upstream bandwidth" simply don't belong in our vocabulary!

The truth is that a home network doesn't really have to be difficult or complex. You don't have to join some geek squad or spend hours learning a new language to successfully create a functioning home network. In fact, you'll find that the project is fairly simple and pretty satisfying.

## What Networks Really Are

So just what is a network, anyway? And how does a home network compare to an office network?

These are both good questions that get right to the heart of the matter. Let's start with the first question.

A network is nothing more than something that provides the means for different things to communicate with each other. You already use one of the world's biggest networks whenever you make a telephone call. Your phone number is the key that enables other people to pick up their phone, dial your number, and talk to you from virtually anywhere on the planet. Computer networks function very much like the telephone network because they were actually modeled after the telephone network to a large extent. Figure 1-1 gives you an idea of how home networks function, and Figure 1-2 shows how the telephone network is quite similar.

**Figure 1-1**    A Home Network Connects Your PCs and Other Devices So That They Can Communicate

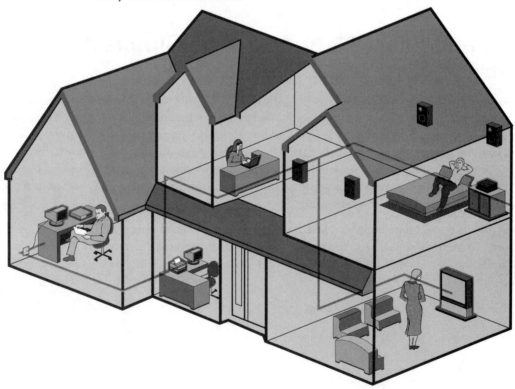

**Figure 1-2**   The Telephone Network Functions Much Like Your Home Network Except on a Larger Scale

It's true that when you use a computer network, you typically aren't expecting another person to be at the other end of the line, but you don't always expect that with the telephone network, either. After all, haven't you ever made a phone call hoping that you would get someone's answering machine instead of talking directly to that person? When you do get the answering machine, you're interacting with that machine in much the same manner as if you were using a typical computer network and the devices on that network. Similar to how two network devices might communicate, the answering machine gives you a message, waits for your response, and then saves your response so that it can be picked up later.

So, if networks aren't all that unfamiliar, it's time to answer the second question regarding how home networks compare to larger networks like those in an office. Actually, the typical home network is very similar to an office network, but in a generally simpler, friendlier, and far less expensive package. That is, a home network still allows your PCs to talk to each other and share things such as files, printers, and Internet connections, but the manufacturers of home networking gear, such as Linksys, have concentrated on reducing the complexity so that you don't have to be an engineer to make it all work. In addition, home networks typically use a much simpler security model that doesn't require you to put up with complications like usernames, passwords, and deciding who gets to share what (unless you want to).

## How Networks Really Work

Computers aren't people, but they still communicate on a network similar to how a group of people communicates. That is, computers send out information that is addressed to a particular individual and then wait for a response that tells them that the message was successfully received. PCs perform this task quickly, and that's part of what makes networks so practical.

To get a better understanding of the process, imagine that Sarah is working on a homework assignment on the PC in her room. When she completes her book report, she needs a printed copy, but she doesn't have a printer connected to her PC. A printer is connected to the PC in the den, and she can use it to print out her report. The conversation between the PCs goes something like this:

"Hello den computer, this is Sarah's PC. I'm sending you this report to print."

"Okay, Sarah's PC, this is the den PC. I received the data and sent it to my printer."

Sure, that exchange sounds trivial, but it does provide a nutshell description of what's going on, as further illustrated by Figure 1-3. At a basic level, a network functions quite simply by sending different messages as needed. The information in those messages—the data—can be something like Sarah's book report, digital images from your recent vacation, music files that you've saved on one of your PCs, or whatever other types of information you want to share.

**Figure 1-3**    The PCs on Your Home Network Talk to Each Other Through the
Network

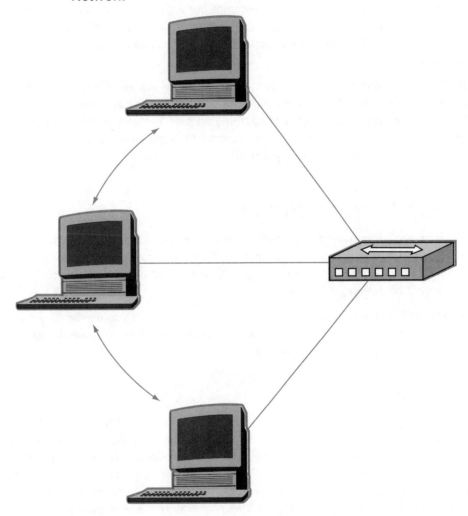

Things are more complicated inside the inner workings of the network. In Sarah's case, for example, the printer and the den PC actually engage in quite a bit of additional conversation, discussing whether the printer is out of paper, how many pages have finished printing so far, and details of what other reports the printer has been asked to print recently. Just like the telephone network, your computer network has to keep track of who is supposed to get each bit of information and make sure that everyone else isn't drowned by a sea of data that's not intended for them. Fortunately, your network automatically handles this additional complication, and you don't have to worry about it.

# A Network Really Isn't Too Complicated for You

Setting up your own home network probably sounds like a great idea, but you might still have some doubts about whether it's really something that you can do. That's understandable, especially if you've heard horror stories about how difficult and complicated anything related to networks can be.

Well, don't believe those stories. The honest truth is that if you're willing to follow some simple directions, you can choose the proper equipment and install your own home network. You can then enjoy the benefits of having your own network without depending on someone else to make sure it all works, and if something goes wrong in the future, you'll know how to fix it. You really can do it yourself!

# Learning How to Share

The basic idea behind networks is something everyone learned in kindergarten or even preschool—sharing. Networks are about sharing. It wouldn't make any sense for you to create a home network if you had only a single PC (and no other network devices) because then there would be nothing to share.

It doesn't matter if you are a single person with multiple PCs or if you live in a house full of people, because the idea is the same. A network makes it far easier to share the assets and resources that are spread across the network.

## Sharing Your Files

Home networks were originally created to make file sharing easier. Prior to the existence of home networks, if you wanted to use a file that was on someone else's computer, you had to go to that person's computer, copy the file to a removable disk (or tape in the really distant past), go back to your computer, and finally copy the file onto your system. This was sometimes called a "sneakernet" because the files were transferred by someone walking around in sneakers. Figure 1-4 gives you an idea of how networking has changed things.

**Figure 1-4** Your Home Network Allows You to Share Files Without Running from Room to Room

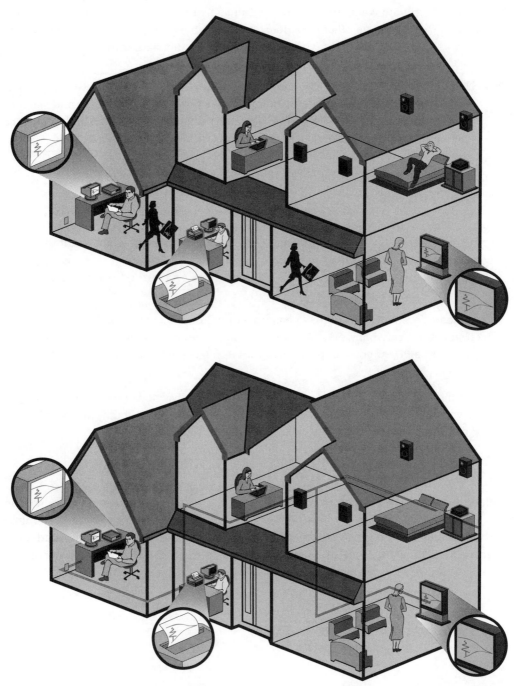

File sharing has never been the same since two or more computers were networked. Now it's almost as easy to open a file stored elsewhere on your network as it is to open one that's right on your PC. If Mom wants to browse through last summer's vacation photos that are stored on the PC in the home office, she doesn't have to bother Dad when he's paying the bills. She can simply use one of the other PCs and have instant access to the shared files.

 **NOTE** Sharing files is an essential step in setting up your home network, and it's something that is easily overlooked in your haste to "get it connected and see if it works." In Chapter 8, "Sharing Your Network," you learn how to share the files that you want other people on your home network to be able to access.

## Sharing Printers

Another great way to take advantage of your home network is by sharing one or more printers. Few home PC users print enough to make a really good printer worthwhile, but it can make a lot of sense to get a better printer that you're going to share. Printing to a network printer is faster and easier than putting your files on a floppy disk and taking them to another PC for printing.

As you will learn in Chapter 8, you have a couple of options to share a printer on your home network. Depending on what works best for your family, you can share a printer that is connected directly to a PC, or you can place that printer in a separate location where it is convenient for everyone to use.

You can even share more than one printer on your home network. For example, you might want to have a laser printer for fast, high-quality text printing and a photo-quality color inkjet for printing graphics.

## Sharing an Internet Connection

One of the newer uses for a home network is to allow everyone to share an Internet connection. This is especially true in homes where a broadband connection such as cable or DSL makes it possible for several people to surf the Web at the same time. Rather than a broadband connection being used by only one person directly connected to it at a time, a shared Internet connection gives everyone access when they want it, as shown in Figure 1-5.

**Figure 1-5** With a Home Network, Everyone Can Share a Broadband Internet Connection

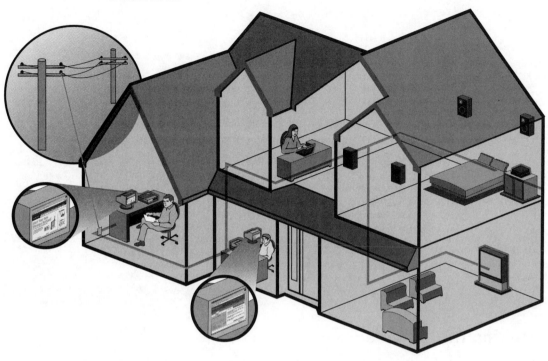

 **TIP** As you'll learn in Chapter 7, "Making Your Network Secure: Locking the Network's Door," it's very important to keep your home network secure from outside attacks. It turns out that the equipment that you use to share an Internet connection can actually make the task of keeping your network secure considerably easier.

The Linksys WRT54G Wireless-G Router shown in Figure 1-6 is an example of the type of equipment you can use to easily and securely share your Internet connection.

**Figure 1-6** A Wireless Router Makes It Easy to Share Your Broadband Internet Connection

## Sharing Multimedia

Regardless of all the other uses for your home network, the one that will ultimately provide you with the most enjoyment will probably be sharing various types of digital media content. You might not realize it yet, but a home network is going to make a big change in the way your family plays.

# Headline: Entertainment Network Wows Friends and Neighbors

If you really want to wow your friends and neighbors, it's hard to beat the effect of a well-thought-out system of entertainment options connected to your home network. Just imagine the possibilities:

- You can have thousands of songs arranged in play lists to match any occasion.

- You can play multiplayer video games via your broadband Internet connection.

- You can listen to countless Internet radio stations in virtually any format around the world.

- You can rent movies for instant viewing without ever leaving your home.

- You (or others) can view your prized exotic fish tank using a wireless webcam.

 **NOTE** You can find out more about the Linksys gear mentioned in this section on the Web at www.linksys.com.

## Home Entertainment Centers

Listening to music has certainly changed over the years. Instead of playing one song or a single disc at a time, PCs have made it easy to set up play lists of your favorite songs so that you never have to play DJ during a party again. Until recently, it simply wasn't very convenient to play music that was stored on your computer through your stereo because most people didn't want a PC in their living room. That all changed with the introduction of products such as the Linksys WMA11B Wireless-B Media Adapter shown in Figure 1-7. This handy device wirelessly bridges the gap between your PC and your stereo to create a home entertainment center.

**Figure 1-7**     A Wireless Media Adapter Channels the Music from Your PC to Your Home Stereo System

# Wireless Game Consoles

Does your home have a video game console such as a Sony PS2 or a Microsoft Xbox? If so, you probably already know that multiplayer games are even more fun than single player games. What you might not know is that by using your broadband Internet connection, you can open up a whole new world of challenging multiplayer games where your opponent might literally be halfway around the world!

The Linksys WGA54G Wireless-G game adapter shown in Figure 1-8 can be the key to connecting your video game console to the Internet through your home network.

**Figure 1-8**     A Wireless Game Adapter Connects Your Video Game Console to the Internet

# Internet Radio

The Internet can be an amazing source of entertainment. In addition to millions of websites, another part of the Internet exists of which you might not be aware. Radio stations all over the world broadcast their programs across the Internet for free. You can listen to rock music from New York, opera from Rome, or new age music from Tokyo as easily as listening to your local FM stations on your radio—and without the static! For example, Figure 1-9 shows just a few of the stations that are available in the world music category in Windows Media Player.

**Figure 1-9**    The Whole World Is Within Range When You Listen to Internet Radio Stations

 **TIP**   Remember that your home network's wireless media adapter is just as adept at playing your favorite Internet radio stations on your stereo system as it is at playing music from your PC's play lists.

# Wireless Webcams

If you need one more reason why you'll want your own home network, consider the many different ways you could use a wireless webcam. Earlier I mentioned monitoring your exotic fish tank, but what about some of these ideas:

- Place a wireless camera where you can see who is at your front door on the screen of your PC.

- Set up a webcam so that you can check on the status of your home when you're at work.

- Keep track of your infant's room using a wireless camera.

- Use the motion detection feature of your wireless webcam to record the neighbor's dog when it visits your rose garden.

Figure 1-10 shows the Linksys WVC11B Wireless-B Internet Video Camera. This handy unit might just be the crowning touch for your home network.

**Figure 1-10**    A Wireless Internet Video Camera Enables You to See What's Going on Even if You Can't Be There Yourself

## Working Remotely

Finally, a home network can give you more time at home away from your office. Here are a few ways:

- Save the time of a commute by quickly logging in to the office in emergencies. Check e-mail, get documents, or publish your web pages.

- Attend scheduled meetings virtually from the comfort of your home.

- With a wireless network, work comfortably from the comfort of your own living room, backyard, or porch on a nice sunny day.

# Summary

A network can add a lot of entertainment and convenience to your home. In this chapter, you learned about some of the many things that you can do with your own home network, but that's only the beginning.

In the next chapter, you'll learn the basics of what makes up a home network. After you understand how a network functions, you will have an easier time understanding exactly what you will need to make your home network a reality.

# Things You'll Learn

- The different types of home networks
- The types of hardware you might need for your network
- Basic information about network software

# Chapter 2

# Home Networking Basics

Now that you have some ideas about why you really want your own home network, it's time to take a few minutes to learn the basics of how networks work. This rudimentary information will help you make the right choices to best suit your needs.

## The Two Flavors of Home Networks

Home networks come in two basic flavors—wired and wireless. Each has its own advantages as well as disadvantages. Depending on your situation, you might find that a wired network fits your needs, or you might want to opt for a wireless network. It's even possible that you'll want some combination of the two. The equipment—printers, webcams, game consoles, and home entertainment centers—discussed in Chapter 1, "Why You Want Your Own Network," plugs into either the wired or wireless hardware framework described in this chapter.

### Wired Networks

A *wired* network is one where each computer is connected to the network through a cable, as shown in Figure 2-1. These cables typically look like a slightly fatter than normal telephone cable. Until fairly recently, wired networks were the only available option.

**Figure 2-1**    Wired Networks Require Cables to Each PC

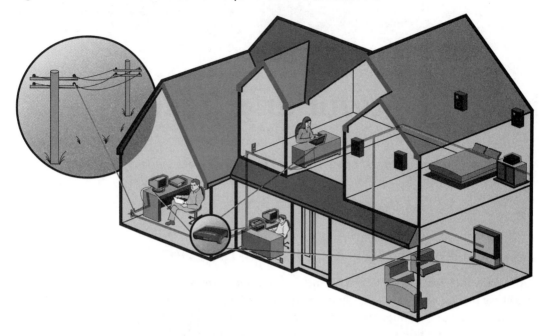

Wired networks offer several advantages:

- ■ The equipment for a wired network is inexpensive.

- ■ Many computers built in the past few years have a wired network adapter built in.

- ■ Wired networks move information somewhat faster than wireless networks.

- ■ Wired networks are generally more secure than wireless networks because they are harder to access physically.

On the other hand, wired networks have some disadvantages, too:

- ■ Running the wires from room to room can be difficult.

- ■ Network cables can look messy.

- ■ Network cables can come loose and cause the connection to fail

- ■ Adding more computers to a wired network might result in unexpected expense if you run out of connections on your network.

All wired networks are not the same. The most common type of wired network is called an *Ethernet* network, and it uses special network cables. Some wired networks make use of the existing telephone wiring or your home's power lines, but telephone line and power line networks are not as popular as the Ethernet network.

 **TIP** Ethernet networks are often referred to as 10BASE-T or 100BASE-T. A newer standard, 1000BASE-T (also called Gigabit), has typically not yet reached the home networking market.

## Wireless Networks

*Wireless* networks use radio signals in place of wires to transmit the information among the devices on your network. Wireless is a relatively recent addition to the networking scene, but it has really taken off—especially in the home networking arena. Figure 2-2 shows how a wireless network might look.

**Figure 2-2** Wireless Networks Communicate Using Radio Signals Rather Than Cables

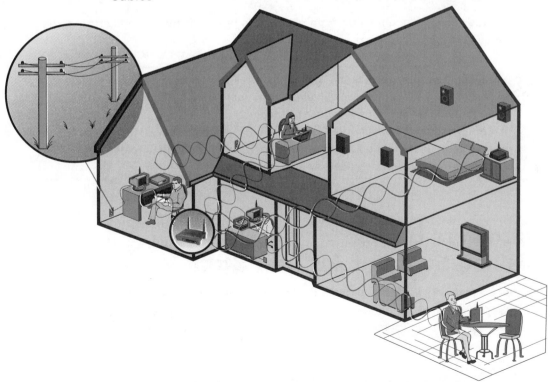

Wireless networks offer several advantages compared to wired networks:

- Installing wireless networks is easier than with wired networks, because you do not have to run cables.

- Adding more PCs to a wireless network is easy.

- Wireless networks give you the freedom to move to different locations within the range of the network with virtually no fuss or bother.

- Wireless networks are rapidly becoming the most popular form of home networking, so the wireless network you set up today might have a longer useful lifetime than a wired network would.

Wireless networks do have some disadvantages, though:

- The basic equipment required to set up a wireless network costs somewhat more than that for a simple wired network.

- Wireless networks tend to be slower than wired networks.

- Keeping a wireless network secure is somewhat more difficult than with a wired network.

- Wireless networks can suffer from interference from numerous sources, such as microwave ovens and cordless phones.

- Wireless networks might suffer from obstruction problems that severely restrict their operating distance.

 **NOTE** The term *Wi-Fi* is often used for wireless networks. This term refers to wireless networks that meet certain standards, such as 802.11b, 802.11a, and 802.11g, so that equipment from various manufacturers can be used together. In Chapter 3, "Choosing the Best Network Type," you will learn more about how to decide which type of network will best suit your needs and how these wireless networking standards affect your choices.

# Hardware Basics: Making Sense of All That Stuff

To create a network, you need to begin by adding certain types of hardware. If you're new to networks, you might find the various pieces a little confusing. In an effort to reduce the confusion level, the next sections explain the basics of network hardware.

# Network Adapters

Each PC on the network needs a *network adapter* to enable it to connect to the network. In some cases, a network adapter is already built in to the PC; however, this is not always true. Unfortunately, in some cases, you might also find that your PC includes a network adapter but, not the correct type for your choice of network. For example, you might want to create a wireless network, it's but your PC contains a built-in Ethernet adapter. If so, you can still install a wireless home network—you'll simply have to add a wireless network adapter to your PC.

It's often difficult to tell, especially with notebook computers, which network adapters, if any, are present. Notebooks might contain built-in wired adapters, wireless adapters, neither, or both! You might have to check your owner's manual or the specification sheet that came with your system to determine what you have. Most modern PCs will include at least one type of network adapter.

 **TIP** Network adapters are sometimes called NICs—which is an acronym for network interface cards.

Choosing the correct type of network adapter is an important first step in ensuring a successful home network. Choosing the correct hardware is covered in depth in Chapter 4, "Selecting Network Hardware: Your Complete Buying Guide," but for now it is probably most important for you to remember that wired and wireless networks use different types of network adapters. Figure 2-3 shows one type of network adapter you might choose for a wired network, and Figure 2-4 shows an adapter you might choose for a wireless network.

**Figure 2-3**   Network Adapter for Your Desktop PC for Use on a Wired Network

**Figure 2-4**    Network Adapter for Your Desktop PC for Use on a Wireless Network

 **CAUTION**    Desktop PCs and laptop PCs typically use different types of network adapters, so it is important to choose adapters that are compatible with the type of PC you use. Laptops use PC Cards, which fit into a special slot from the outside. Desktops use PCI Cards, which are inserted into slots inside the computer while it's powered off.

## Hubs

The data that travels across a network generally goes through a central point to be redistributed as needed. The simplest device for this purpose is called a *hub*.

Your local office supply store might sell network hubs, but you will probably want to steer away from hubs because you pay a price in terms of network performance for that simplicity.

 **TIP**    Hubs and switches are used only on wired networks.

# Switches

A *switch* is a device that is quite similar to a hub, but with the added advantage of better performance. In most cases, a switch, such as the Linksys EZXS55W EtherFast 10/100 5-port Auto-Sensing Switch shown in Figure 2-5, costs only a little more than a comparable hub.

**Figure 2-5**    A Switch Controls the Traffic on Your Network

 **TIP**    Although it is less expensive in the long run to buy a switch with enough connections for the number of PCs you'll want to connect to your network, you can connect two switches together to add additional connections to your network.

# Routers

A *router* is the next step up from a switch. In fact, most routers have a switch built in to the router. The primary difference between a switch and a router is that a router is used to connect two different networks and to control how much of each network is visible to the other network. In most cases, one of those networks is the Internet and the other network is your home network.

Routers serve a very important function by providing a *firewall* between your home network and the Internet. This means that other people who are browsing the Internet are prevented from viewing or modifying your personal files that are on your home computers. Firewalls and security are discussed in detail in Chapter 7, "Making Your Network Secure: Locking the Network's Door."

**TIP**   Routers are used on both wired and wireless networks. Some routers and gateways have a built-in switch so that they support both wireless and wired devices on the same network.

Figure 2-6 shows a very popular router, the Linksys BEFSR41 EtherFast Cable/DSL Router with 4-Port Switch.

**Figure 2-6**       Linksys BEFSR41 EtherFast Cable/DSL Router with 4-Port Switch

**TIP**   Even though the Linksys BEFSR41 is called a *Cable/DSL* router, it also works with other types of Internet connections, such as fixed wireless.

## Access Points

An *access point* provides the access that enables wireless devices to communicate with the wired portion of your network. In most cases, a wireless router is a better choice for your home network than an access point because the access point does not offer all the features of a wireless router. You will learn more about this in Chapter 4.

## Gateways

A *gateway* is essentially a router with a built-in cable modem. In some cases, gateways include more advanced firewall features than routers, but this is not always true.

# Software Basics: Details Only a Geek Could Love

Computers are tools, but they're unlike most other types of tools in a very important way. The difference between computers and other types of tools is that most tools are designed to do specific types of tasks, whereas computers can be reprogrammed for many different tasks simply by changing the software that they run.

PCs were not originally designed with networking in mind, but through the addition of a number of software components, networking is now a reality. This network software is what enables your PC to communicate with other computers and makes your home network possible. Networking software is packaged as an integral part of modern PC operating systems such as Windows—which is used for the examples in this book—as well as Mac OS and Linux.

Networking software is different from most of the software that you use on your PC because of the type of job that it does. When you use a spreadsheet program or a word processor, you're well aware of the application that you're using. With networking software, that's not the case, because the networking software runs in the background providing a service without coming to the foreground to say, "Here I am."

Two primary elements make up the networking software on your PC—the *client* and the *protocols* (the terminology you'll see when setting up a Windows-based network). The sections that follow provide more details on these two components.

## Network Clients

The network client is a piece of software that provides your PC with access to the network's services. For a typical home network, this software is known as the Client for Microsoft Networks.

 **NOTE**  Most PCs also load a second client called File and Printer Sharing for Microsoft Networks so that they will be able to share files and printers on the network. This second client is not required to use a network, but without it, you lose most of the reasons for having a network.

# Protocols and Drivers

The next important piece of the networking software puzzle is known as a protocol. The protocol can be thought of as the language that the computers on the network use to communicate with each other. Over the years, hundreds of different protocols have been developed for computer networking, each for its own specific purposes.

Fortunately, in home networking today, things are generally simpler because the industry has standardized on a set of protocols called TCP/IP (Transmission Control Protocol/Internet Protocol)). If TCP/IP sounds vaguely familiar, it's because TCP/IP is the protocol set most commonly used on the Internet (as well as your wired or wireless home network).

Even though having the proper network clients and protocols installed on your PC is vital to successfully creating your home network, the task of making sure the correct software is installed isn't nearly as ominous as it might sound because modern PC operating systems include wizards to automate the process.

Figure 2-7 shows how network clients and protocols are used to allow your PCs to communicate over your network.

**Figure 2-7**    Both the Proper Network Clients and Protocols Are Necessary for a Functioning Network

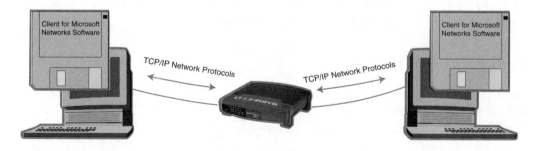

 **NOTE**  The network adapter also requires *driver* software to support the protocols, but this typically is automatically installed as soon as your PC recognizes that the hardware has been installed.

# Summary

In this chapter, you learned that you can have a traditional wired network, a wireless network, or a combination of the two. You learned that each type of network has some strengths and some weaknesses that you should consider when choosing your home network. You saw that various pieces of hardware are necessary to create a network and that a network also has a software component. At this point, you have a basic understanding of how a network functions so that you can move on and start making some choices.

# Part II  Starting Your Network

This part provides the real meat of creating your home network. In four chapters, you learn how to choose, install, and configure your home network.

# Things You'll Learn

- Getting just what you need
- Making your network type selection
- Finding the right wired or wireless equipment

# Chapter 3

# Choosing the Best Network Type

With the basics of what makes up a network out of the way, it's time to move on and choose the best type of network to suit your needs. In many ways, this can be a subjective process because you might find that you prefer one type of network rather than another regardless of objective criteria. There's nothing wrong with taking that approach as long as you're armed with the facts, so that's what this chapter is all about.

## What Do You "Need"?

There's no question that knowing what you really need before you go shopping is important. When you know what you need, you aren't as likely to end up being pressured into buying inappropriate (or even incompatible) equipment, and you're far less likely to walk out of the store minus an absolutely vital piece you need to actually make the network function.

You'll need to know the type of network you want in your home before you can choose the proper network hardware, of course. But you should go beyond that question and consider some additional points to make sure that you end up with the proper mix:

- Will you be connecting your network to the Internet? If so, you'll very likely want some type of router or gateway to make that connection.

- Do you plan to add more PCs (or other equipment) to your network in the future? If so, you should choose a solution that has some additional capacity beyond what you need today.

- Are you going to use your network to supply home entertainment needs? If so, remember that multimedia content—and especially video—can make some heavy demands on the network's capacity, so network throughput (the amount of data the network can handle at one time) becomes very important.

- Is a move to a different home on your horizon? If so, consider how easy it will be to pick up and move your network to a new location.

# Wired or Wireless? That Is the Question

The previous chapter introduced some of the differences between wired and wireless networks. You learned that both types of networks function in a similar manner and that each offers certain advantages. Now it's time to decide if your home network will primarily use cables or radio waves.

Figure 3-1 shows a typical layout for a wired home network. Each device on the network is connected to a switch or router by way of a cable.

**Figure 3-1**      Every Device on a Wired Network Must Have a Cable Connecting It to the Network

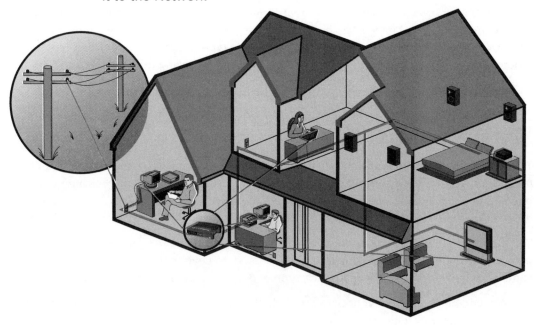

Figure 3-2 shows how a typical wireless network compares to the wired network. Notice that the freedom from that jumble of cables can cause some nasty surprises if you aren't careful. Your neighbor (or a wandering hacker) might become a benefactor of the time and money you've put into your wireless home network. See Chapter 7, "Making Your Network Secure: Locking the Network's Door," for more information on how to prevent these nasty surprises.

**Figure 3-2** Wireless Networks Don't Need Cables, but You Do Need to Control Who Can Access Them

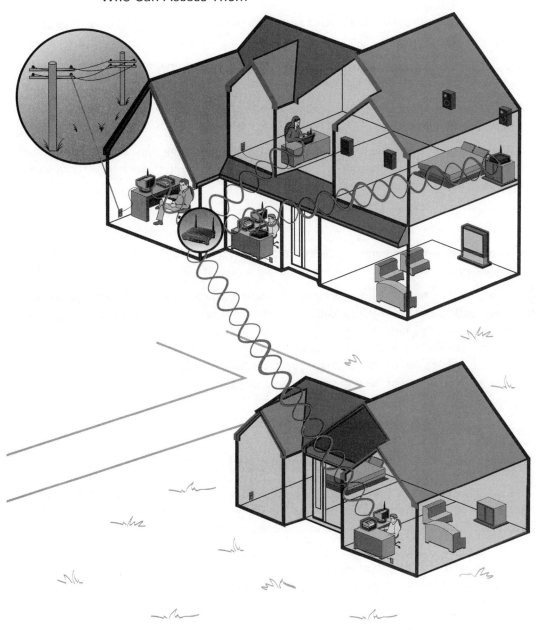

So how do you decide which type of network is best for your home? The best method might be to consider the following points

- If you simply can't stand the idea of any more wires hanging off the backs of your PCs, go wireless.

- If you intend to deliver streaming video to your home entertainment system, a wired network is likely to provide higher-quality pictures and sound.

- If you want the freedom to sit outside on your patio while surfing the Internet on your laptop, go wireless.

- If you aren't comfortable learning how to configure the more detailed security options that wireless entails, you should probably avoid installing a wireless network or find an experienced friend or family member to help you.

- If you're willing to trade a little bit of performance and cost for a bunch of convenience, a wireless network might be for you.

The choice between wired and wireless networks is not necessarily an either/or option; you can have some of both if you're willing to put up with just a little extra complication.

You can probably think of a number of other reasons why a wired or a wireless network is your best option. Whatever you decide, remember that sometimes it's best to simply make a choice and get on with it instead of fretting over every possible minor issue. You should do your homework to make certain that the equipment you choose will be compatible with your PCs, but that's not a difficult task given the advice you find in this book, through online sources, or even in one of the popular computer magazines.

# Wired Networks: Making the Right Connections

A wired network uses cables to make the connections between the devices on the network. Each of the several different types of wired networks uses very specific types of network adapters, cables, switches, and so on to complete those connections.

 **CAUTION** The cables and other components used for different types of wired networking are not interchangeable. You cannot substitute different types of components because they simply will not work.

The sections that follow examine the most common types of wired home networks. These sections will not cover direct PC-to-PC connections using serial cables, parallel cables, USB cables, or IEEE-1394 (FireWire) cables, because these options are very limited and do not provide practical networking capabilities.

## Ethernet Networks

Ethernet networks are far and away the most common type of networking both in the home and in the office. As Figure 3-1 illustrated earlier, an Ethernet network connects the PCs (or other devices such as printers and media hubs) by way of a central hub or switch. Ethernet networks typically provide the highest performance compared to any other type of home networking.

To complete your Ethernet network, you will need the following items:

- **An Ethernet network adapter in each PC**—This might be built in, or it might be a Linksys LNE100TX EtherFast 10/100 LAN Card for a desktop system, a Linksys PCM100 EtherFast 10/100 Integrated PC Card for a laptop, or a Linksys USB200M EtherFast USB 2.0 10/100 Network Adapter that plugs into a USB port on either a desktop or laptop system. Be sure to check each PC to see if it has a built-in Ethernet adapter before creating your shopping list.

- **A network hub, switch, or router with enough ports (ports are receptacles for network cables, like jacks for stereo wires or electrical wall outlets for power cords) so that each device on the network will have its own port**—A hub such as the Linksys EW5HUB Ethernet 5-Port Workgroup Hub or a switch such as the Linksys EZXS55W EtherFast 10/100 5-port Auto-Sensing Switch might be a good option for a network that does not share a broadband Internet connection. If you intend to share a broadband Internet connection, you will want a router such as the Linksys BEFSR41 EtherFast Cable/DSL Router with 4-Port Switch.

- **A Category 5 (commonly called Cat5) or, preferably, Cat5E cable long enough to reach from each PC to the hub, switch, or router**—Recommended practice is to buy cables that are longer than you think you'll need to allow the cables to be neatly laid along the baseboards where they will be less of a hazard.

## Phone Line Networks

At first glance, using your existing telephone lines for networking seems like the perfect solution. Instead of messy-looking cables strung out between all your PCs, you simply plug a telephone cord between your PC and the closest wall jack. (See Figure 3-3.)

**Figure 3-3**     Phone Line Networking Uses Your Existing Telephone Wiring

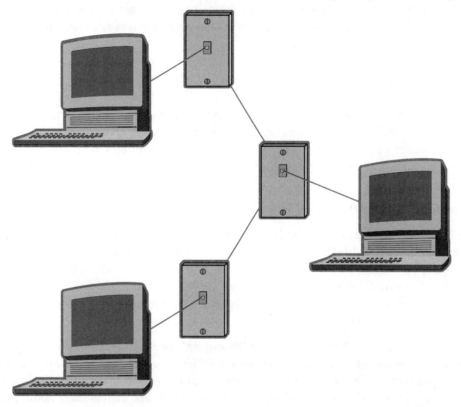

Unfortunately, phone line networking isn't quite the ideal solution that it seems. Phone line networking is relatively slow and might require considerable telephone jack rewiring in some cases—especially if you have to add new jacks to an older home. In addition, unlike an Ethernet network, different brands of phone line networking equipment are unlikely to work together, so you can't mix and match brands. Finally, phone line networking has gone through several versions and simply hasn't caught on with the public, so you might have limited expansion options in the future if you choose this type of network.

Phone line networks don't require a lot of equipment. Here's a list of what you'll need:

■ Each PC will need a phone line network adapter such as the Linksys HPN200 HomeLink Phoneline 10M Network Card. You can also buy the HPN200SK starter kit that contains two of the network adapters.

- A telephone cable long enough to reach from the PC to the nearest telephone jack.

- If you want to connect your phone line network to a cable or DSL Internet connection, you will also need a router such as the Linksys HPRO200 HomeLink PhoneLine 10M Cable/DSL Router. This is not necessary if you don't intend to share an Internet connection.

## Power Line

Like phone line networking, power line networking uses existing wiring in your home so that you do not need to run a bunch of cables between rooms. (See Figure 3-4.) In this case, the signal is transmitted using the electrical wiring in your home.

**Figure 3-4**    Power Line Networking Uses Your Home's Existing Electrical Wiring

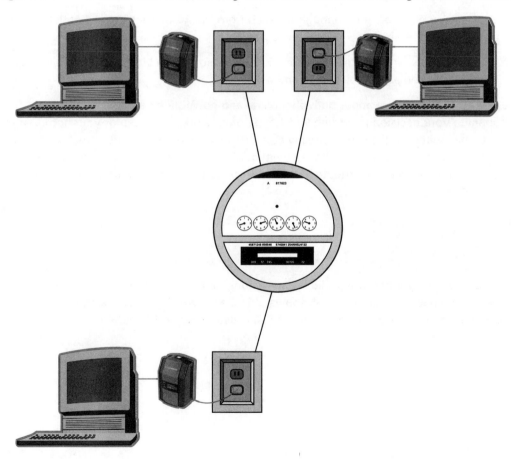

Power line networking shares many of the characteristics of phone line networking. In both cases, a number of tradeoffs result from using existing wiring that was not designed (or installed) with data transfers in mind. Power line networking can be a little faster than phone line networking, but the difference is small, and throughput is still far less than for an Ethernet network. Your home will probably have electrical outlets in virtually every room, though, so it's less likely that you'll need to do any rewiring for power line networking. Power line networking is popular in many European countries, but it has not drawn much interest in the U.S. market to date.

Power line networks are similar to phone line networks in the amount of equipment that you need:

- Each PC needs an adapter such as the Linksys PLUSB10 Instant PowerLine USB Adapter.

- Every PC needs a port of the correct type (in this example, USB).

- You need a USB cable long enough to reach from the PC to the electrical outlet where the Instant PowerLine USB Adapter is located.

- If you want to share an Internet connection, you also need a Linksys PLEBR10 Instant PowerLine EtherFast 10/100 Bridge and a router.

There is an additional fact about both phone line and power line networking that might be important to your decision regarding which type of networking is best for your home. At the current time, neither of these two directly supports devices other than PCs (such as media hubs and wireless webcams), so choosing either of these options will limit your ability to use your home network to distribute multimedia content to an entertainment center or TV.

# Wireless Options: Deciphering the Protocol Soup

Wireless networks use two-way radio transmissions to transfer data between the various devices on the network. As Figure 3-5 shows, this makes wireless networking very attractive for a home network where unsightly cables can cause many problems.

**Figure 3-5**    Wireless Networks Use Invisible Radio Waves in Place of Wires

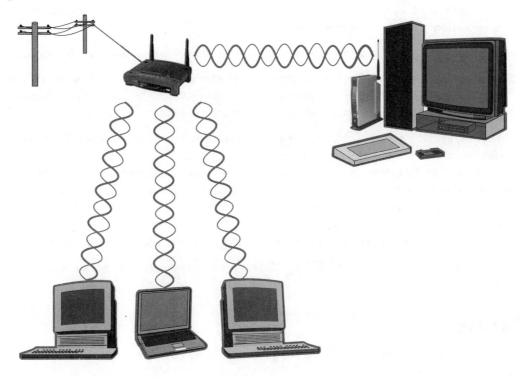

A wireless network can function in two different modes:

- **Ad-hoc mode**—This mode does not use a central device such as a router or access point, and the PCs communicate directly with each other. Ad-hoc mode can save you the cost of an access point or a router, but it makes it more difficult to connect wired and wireless sections of your network.

- **Infrastructure mode**—This mode uses a router or access point to handle all network traffic and makes it possible to access a wired network such as the Internet. In most cases, infrastructure mode is the better choice for your home network.

Wireless networks use the following types of equipment:

- A wireless network adapter for each PC. Some laptop PCs now come with built-in wireless adapters.

- Access points, which provide a central connection between your wireless devices and also to a wired network such as the Internet. If you use an access point, each PC is responsible for its own security unless the wired part of your network is connected to the Internet through a router.

- Wireless routers, which provide built-in security features in addition to the functions of an access point. For most wireless home networks, a wireless router is a better choice than a simple access point would be.

- Wireless gateways, which are essentially wireless routers with a built-in cable modem.

- Wireless Ethernet bridges, game adapters and media adapters that are specialty devices that allow wired equipment to access your wireless network. Chapter 9, "The Magic of Entertainment Options," discusses the use of these types of equipment.

Wireless networking equipment comes in several different flavors, which are defined by the various standards that have been developed to ensure that a degree of compatibility will exist between products from different manufacturers. Some equipment supports more than one of the standards, but most wireless networking gear complies with a single standard. It is very important that you choose the best standard to suit your needs, and that all the equipment you purchase supports that standard. Also, look for the Wi-Fi Certified label, because this indicates that the equipment has been tested and certified to meet the standards.

The next few sections look at the various wireless networking standards to see how they compare.

## 802.11b

The oldest type of wireless networking equipment uses the 802.11b standard, which has the following characteristics:

- Uses the 2.4-GHz unlicensed radio band that is shared with microwave ovens and some cordless phones

- Offers up to 11-Mbps throughput (depending on distance and number of devices)

- Has approximately 100- to 150-foot range indoors (depending on obstructions)

- Can experience radio interference from some cordless phones and from microwave ovens

- Is the most widely adopted wireless networking standard and, therefore, generally the least expensive

## 802.11a

The next type of wireless networking equipment to appear was that complying with the 802.11a standard. The equipment that follows this standard has these characteristics:

- Uses the 5-GHz unlicensed radio band

- Offers up to 54-Mbps throughput (depending on the number of devices)

- Has approximately 25- to 75-foot range indoors (depending on obstructions)

- Is fairly immune to interference because few devices use this radio band

- Is usually more expensive than other options

## 802.11g

The 802.11g standard is currently the newest wireless networking option. This standard has the following characteristics:

- Uses the 2.4-GHz unlicensed radio band

- Offers up to 54-Mbps throughput (or higher, using certain types of equipment with proprietary technology)

- Has approximately 100- to 150-foot range indoors (depending on obstructions)

- Can experience interference from cordless phones and microwave ovens, in addition to some other types of devices

- Is compatible with 802.11b equipment at 11 Mbps, and is only slightly more expensive than 802.11b

Of these three standards, it appears as though 802.11g offers the best mix of performance and value at this time. Identifying 802.11g gear is easy because most manufacturers prominently display some variation such as G or 54G in the product names.

 **TIP**    Chapter 8, "Sharing Your Network," covers how you can inexpensively extend your 802.11b or 802.11g wireless network's range.

## Bluetooth

You might have heard of another wireless standard known as *Bluetooth*. Although Bluetooth also shares the unlicensed 2.4-GHz radio band, it is incompatible with any of the wireless networking standards. It is possible to use Bluetooth for some limited forms of file sharing, but it is really not intended as a type of wireless networking. Rather, Bluetooth is more commonly used for connecting GPS receivers to laptops or PDAs, for wireless headsets for cell phones, and for synchronizing PDAs with desktop PCs. Both the performance and range of Bluetooth are too low to be considered a practical wireless networking option.

# What Went Wrong: Your Quick Fix Reference

Before moving on, it is important to consider some potential trouble spots that could trip you up:

- When buying cables for your Ethernet network, it's very easy to end up with a cable that looks fine but simply won't work. Make sure that all of your network cables are *straight through* (or *patch*) cables rather than *crossover* cables. Crossover cables look just like patch cables but cannot be used for most purposes.

- Buy high-quality cables rather than bargain basement ones. Look for the designation Cat5E rather than Cat5 if you want the best performance from your network. This designation is printed on the side of the cable, usually every few feet along its length.

- Although the wireless networking standards are supposed to be compatible among different brands of equipment, any proprietary extensions to the standards such as the Linksys SpeedBooster technology are not. If you mix equipment that does not include these extensions into a wireless network that has the extensions, you'll lose the benefit of the extensions.

- A phone line network might not work if your telephone jacks are wired improperly. Radio Shack sells an inexpensive phone line tester that you might want to use to check your wiring before you decide on a phone line network.

- Power line networks typically have problems reaching all rooms in a home because of the way electrical circuits are wired. This is a problem that does not have a simple solution, so you might need to move one or more PCs to different rooms to make a power line network function properly.

# Summary

In this chapter, you learned about the different types of home networks. You should now have a fairly good feel for the type of network that will work best for you. In the next chapter, you will learn how to choose the specific equipment you need for your home network.

# Things You'll Learn

- Balancing network costs and performance
- Understanding the influence of your Internet connection
- Choosing the right wired network components
- Selecting the proper wireless network components
- Creating a mixed network

# Chapter 4

# Selecting Network Hardware: Your Complete Buying Guide

It's finally time to start putting together your shopping list. Buying the proper equipment is very important because doing so will allow you to concentrate on more important things rather than having to make multiple trips to the store buying more equipment (or returning useless gear). In this chapter, you will learn about the specific items that you will need to make your home network a reality.

 NOTE The computer industry continues to develop newer and better products at a rapid pace. This is equally true in the area of home networking, and you might discover that a specific product model that is mentioned in this chapter has been replaced by a newer model. If so, there's no reason for alarm because the newer model will certainly serve as well as the version that it replaced. New home network gear typically improves on the performance, security, ease of use, or cost of the prior generation—sometimes all of the above!

## Cost Versus Performance Considerations: It's Your Money

In shopping for your home networking equipment, you have several things to consider. One of the most important considerations is directly related to how much value you will get for the money that you spend. You probably don't have an unlimited budget, and you most likely don't want to waste a lot of money on needless expenditures.

Here are a few last-minute considerations to keep in mind as you balance the various factors in deciding which equipment to purchase for your home network:

- Wireless networking equipment tends to cost a bit more than wired network equipment, but wireless networks are easier and possibly less expensive to install—especially if you would need to hire someone to run cables for a wired network.

- 802.11g (54 Mbps) wireless networking equipment is a bit more expensive than 802.11b (11 Mbps) equipment, but it offers nearly five times the performance in the home. 802.11a equipment is even more expensive than 802.11g equipment, but it offers no better performance and shorter range, so it's generally not a good choice for your home network.

- Some of your PCs might already have built-in networking hardware. If so, using those capabilities can save you money if you make certain that any new equipment that you purchase is compatible with the built-in hardware. You might want to use the wired switch contained in some wireless routers to connect PCs that are close to the router to save some money, because wired network adapters are typically cheaper than wireless adapters.

- Manufacturers often produce different lines of networking hardware. Choosing the home-oriented line will almost certainly save you considerable money compared to the industrial-level equipment meant for business usage.

# Making Sure It All Works Together: It Depends on Your Connections

It's probably safe to assume that if you want to set up a home network, you have some type of Internet connection available. If you do, one of the purposes for installing your home network is probably to allow that Internet connection to be shared on your network. This sharing of an Internet connection has a direct influence on your choice for at least one piece of your network hardware.

Several different types of Internet connections are available. You might have one or more of the following options:

- DSL (Digital Subscriber Line)
- Cable
- Broadband wireless
- Satellite
- Dialup (Public Switched Telephone Network)

Both the DSL and dialup options use the telephone lines that come into your home, but they do so in very different ways. Dialup is available anywhere that a standard phone works, although DSL is available only in areas within a certain distance from a telephone company facility known as a *central office*. Cable access uses the same cable that provides cable TV. Wireless Internet is the newest option of the group and uses radio waves to supply the connection. Wireless Internet connections are far less common than the other options, but they make it possible to get broadband connections in areas that are not served by DSL or cable.

 **NOTE** Satellite Internet connections are also available, but their higher cost and lower performance make them a less attractive option except in areas where no other type of broadband connection is available.

Each type of Internet connection requires its own method of connecting your PCs to the Internet. In the case of a dialup connection, the device that makes this connection is a *modem,* and it connects directly to a PC either by plugging into an *expansion slot* (internal modem) or through a *serial port* (external modem) on your PC. Some PCs have built-in modems.

 **NOTE** See Chapter 8, "Sharing Your Network," for more information on sharing an Internet connection.

In most cases other than for a dialup connection, the device that makes the connection to the Internet (such as a cable or DSL modem) provides an Ethernet port for connecting to a PC or to your network. Typically, you connect this Ethernet port to a router, which then provides the firewall and Internet connection-sharing services for your network. Figure 4-1 shows how the router sits between your home network and the Internet to help prevent unauthorized access to your files.

**Figure 4-1    A Router Helps Protect Your Home Network from Outside Access**

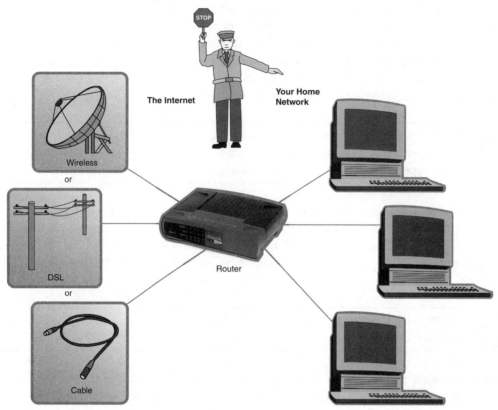

If you have a cable connection, you might want to consider buying a unit that combines the cable modem and a router in a single box. For example, Figure 4-2 shows the Linksys WCG200 Wireless-G Cable Gateway. (Linksys also makes the BEFCMU10 EtherFast Cable Modem with USB and Ethernet Connection for wired networks.) This type of combination device is especially useful if your cable company charges rent for your cable modem and it allows you to buy your own compatible unit.

**Figure 4-2**     This Gateway Combines a Cable Modem and a Wireless Router in a Single Package

If you do not need a built-in cable modem, you will find that whichever router you choose will work with any of the common broadband connections.

**NOTE**   It is possible to set up your network without a router and use one of your PCs to control the shared Internet connection, but skipping the router often leads to problems. See Chapter 8 for more information on the subject.

# Wired Network Hardware: The Nuts and Bolts

Now it is time to turn your attention to the specific devices you will need if you have decided upon a wired Ethernet network. In some ways, wired networks require a bit more advance planning than do wireless networks because a wired network must have a place for each PC or other network device to plug into the network. If you run out of ports before you run out of PCs, you'll either need to expand the network's capacity or leave some of your PCs disconnected—not exactly the ideal situation.

**TIP**   If you do run out of ports on your wired router, you can plug a switch into one of the router's ports and then use the ports on the switch to expand your network. It is not necessary to add a second router for this purpose. A switch is also ideal for adding additional ports at a location some distance from the router—such as the opposite end of the house—because you will need only a single network cable between the router and the switch.

## Choosing a Router

Choosing the correct router for your wired home network is actually not too difficult. Linksys makes several different models that are appropriate for a home network, including the BEFSR41 EtherFast Cable/DSL Router with 4-Port Switch shown in Figure 4-3.

Figure 4-3    The BEFSR41 Router Incorporates a 4-Port Switch

If you need more than the four ports offered by the BEFSR41, the Linksys BEFSR81 is a good choice with its eight ports. If you already have a switch, consider the BEFSR11 with its single port. Routers with more than eight ports are available but designed mainly for businesses; they are rarely found in today's home networks.

Each of the BEFSR line of routers includes a number of important features beyond basic sharing and firewall support. These include *network address translation (NAT)* to hide your PCs from direct Internet access and automatic configuration for your networked PCs.

## Choosing Network Adapters

Many PCs have built-in network adapters so they do not need to have an adapter added. If you aren't sure about your PCs, you might want to check on this before you make up your shopping list. One foolproof method of checking is to look at the back panel of the PC to see if it has a jack similar to a standard phone jack but wider than a standard phone jack. (Try plugging in a modular phone cord to be sure—the modular phone cord plug won't snap into the larger network cable jack.) The network jack is an RJ45 jack, and a phone jack is an RJ11 jack. You can also check the owner's manual.

If you need to purchase network adapters, you might want to consider several options. Figure 4-4 shows the most common type of network adapter that is used in desktop PCs. In this case, the adapter that is shown is the Linksys LNE100TX EtherFast 10/100 LAN Card.

**Figure 4-4**    A Network Adapter Card for Desktop PCs

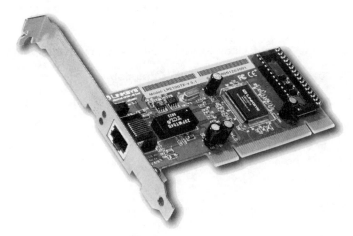

Laptop PCs require a different type of adapter card. Figure 4-5 shows the Linksys PCM100 EtherFast 10/100 Integrated PC Card (credit card-sized, but thicker) that you might choose for laptop use.

**Figure 4-5**    A Network Adapter Card for Laptop PCs

 **TIP**   Make sure all the wired network adapters you buy say either 10/100 or 100 to ensure the best possible network performance.

If any of the following situations apply, you might want to consider another type of wired network adapter that plugs into a USB port on your PC and provides a jack for a standard Ethernet cable:

- You are afraid to open your desktop PC to install a network adapter card.

- Your laptop PC doesn't have an available PC Card slot.

- You want the flexibility of being able to connect any PC to your network without installing anything in the PC.

Figure 4-6 shows an example of this type of adapter, the Linksys USB200M Compact USB 2.0 10/100 Network Adapter.

**Figure 4-6**     A Network Adapter That Plugs into a USB Port

 **NOTE**   USB network adapters typically offer lower performance than other types of wired network adapters. For maximum performance from a USB network adapter, make certain that it is USB 2.0 compatible (like the Linksys USB200M) and that you plug it into a USB 2.0 port. The USB 1.1 ports found on older PCs do not permit full-speed network operations.

Don't forget that you'll also need the proper network cables for your wired network. It's a good idea to always buy cables that are somewhat longer than you think that you will need, because a cable that is too short isn't going to stretch. Look for cables labeled Cat5E—you'll find them in the same area of the store as the rest of the networking equipment.

# Wireless Network Hardware: Nuts, Bolts, and Waves

Wireless networks are somewhat easier to install than wired networks. They're also a bit easier to plan because you can usually add more PCs or other devices to a wireless network without worrying about running out of available ports.

 **NOTE** To keep things just a bit easier on you, the wireless networking selections throughout the remainder of this book are based on the 802.11g standard. This equipment generally provides the best blend of performance, cost, and compatibility; 802.11g has also become the de facto standard in wireless equipment being developed and evolved these days.

## Choosing a Wireless Router

A wireless router connects to your Internet connection and allows your PCs and the other devices on your network to communicate. You have several excellent choices, including the Linksys WRT54GS Wireless-G Broadband Router with SpeedBooster shown in Figure 4-7.

**Figure 4-7** The Linksys WRT54GS Wireless-G Broadband Router Is One of the Highest Performance Wireless Routers You Can Buy

In planning your wireless network, it's worth trying to look for the Linksys SpeedBooster models whenever possible. The SpeedBooster technology, which is available only from Linksys, offers much higher performance than standard 802.11g equipment does. SpeedBooster from Linksys can achieve a 35-percent speed improvement over regular 802.11g if all the wireless adapters and gateways use SpeedBooster. You can still get a 20-percent boost among SpeedBooster equipment on a network that mixes SpeedBooster and 802.11g gear, but no improvement at all if you're using older 802.11b devices on that network. Some other manufacturers offer their own proprietary performance-boosting technologies, but they don't work with competing products, either.

## Choosing Wireless Network Adapters

As is the case with wired network adapters, you should begin your wireless network adapter shopping by first determining if any of your PCs already have wireless networking capabilities built in. Generally speaking, this capability is not often included in desktop PCs, but you might find it in newer laptop PCs.

Figure 4-8 shows the most common type of wireless network adapter for desktop PCs. This Linksys WMP54GS Wireless-G PCI Adapter with SpeedBooster model features a detachable antenna so that you can move or replace the antenna if necessary. See Chapter 8 for more information on wireless network antenna options.

**Figure 4-8**      A Wireless Network Adapter for Desktop PCs

If your laptop PC needs a wireless network adapter, you might want to consider the Linksys WPC54GS Wireless-G Notebook Adapter with SpeedBooster shown in Figure 4-9. If your laptop has an 802.11b adapter built in, switching to this Linksys adapter will likely improve your wireless performance.

**Figure 4-9**    A Wireless Network Adapter for Laptop PCs

As with wired network adapters, you can also find wireless network adapters that plug into a USB port. Figure 4-10 shows the Linksys WUSB54G Wireless-G USB Network Adapter. (At press time, none of the USB wireless network adapters offers the SpeedBooster option.)

**Figure 4-10**    A Wireless Network Adapter That Plugs into a USB Port

## Adding More Access Points

If you have a very large home, you might find that you cannot get a reliable wireless network signal everywhere in the house or outside in your yard. This can also be a problem with certain types of construction where your walls could block the signals. If so, adding an extra access point such as the Linksys WAP54G in the area where you need a better signal provides an excellent solution to the problem.

An access point is similar to a router, but the access point lacks the firewall features that are so important at the point where your home network connects to the Internet. If you already have a router handling this firewall function, it's unnecessary to duplicate that same functionality in an add-on access point.

 **TIP** Even if you don't need to extend the range of your wireless network, adding an access point will improve the network's throughput. This is especially true if you have a mix of Linksys SpeedBooster equipment and other equipment that does not support this technology, because you can assign all the non-SpeedBooster equipment to the access point and leave only the SpeedBooster equipment accessing the router. If you do this, be sure to configure the access point and router using different service set identifiers (SSIDs) and channels. (Be sure to read Chapters 6, 7, and 8 before you attempt this.)

## Adding a Wireless Print Server

This next item is one that won't be needed for all home networks, but it is something that can certainly add a lot of convenience in many situations. A wireless print server such as the Linksys WPS54GU2 Wireless-G PrintServer for USB 2.0 shown in Figure 4-11 enables you to place a printer anywhere you like—like in the hall closet, that unused bedroom, or even in the garage (if it's really noisy)—so that it will be convenient for everyone in your home. Because this means that you won't have to put the printer next to a PC, any family member can use the printer without disturbing anyone else, and you won't have to deal with the clutter from a bunch of printer cables, either.

**Figure 4-11** A Wireless Print Server Enables You to Place a Printer in the Most Convenient Location

The WPS54GU2 supports both standard parallel printers and USB printers. You can even plug one of each into the unit if you have two printers to share.

# Setting Up a Mixed Network: Where Wired Meets Wireless

If you are just a little perplexed at making the decision between a wired and a wireless home network, there's nothing wrong with that. As you have learned, each type of network is the better choice for certain purposes. That's why you might actually decide that part of your home network should be wired and part of it should be wireless. This section provides you with a quick look at how this impacts your equipment choices.

## Wired/Wireless Routers

The first requirement for a mixed wired (Ethernet) and wireless network is that you need to be able to supply a network signal to both wired and wireless devices. Fortunately, this presents no problem because the Linksys WRT54GS Wireless-G Broadband Router recommended earlier (and shown in Figure 4-7) easily handles both tasks. In addition to the wireless access point that is built in to the WRT54GS, the unit also includes a four-port wired switch.

If you already have a wired router—perhaps because you have a broadband cable or DSL connection—and you just want to add some wireless devices to your network, you don't need to replace the existing wired router with a wireless router. In that case, you'll probably want to add a wireless access point such as the Linksys WAP54G Wireless-G Access Point.

 **TIP**  If you're creating a mixed wired and wireless home network, remember to buy the appropriate network adapters for each type of connection.

## Wireless Ethernet Bridges

If you want to set up your home network in two different areas, a wireless network seems ideal because you don't have to string a cable between the two locations. There is just one problem with this scenario—you might discover that you need some wired network connections in both locations. Fortunately, an easy solution to this problem exists that does not require running a really long network cable.

Figure 4-12 shows the solution. It is the Linksys WET54G Wireless-G Ethernet Bridge. This is a device that enables any Ethernet device to connect to your wireless network. That Ethernet device could be a single device or a wired router that connects to several devices. Even better, the WET54G doesn't require drivers, so it can be used with anything that uses an Ethernet connection. You do have to do some minor configuration of the WET54G before you can use it, but that's accomplished easily by following the instructions in the quick start manual.

It is also possible to configure two access points to create a wireless bridge, but doing so limits their ability to be used as access points. By using a dedicated wireless bridge such as the WET54G at one end, your wireless router or access point can continue to function normally, connecting to a number of wireless devices at the same time. The wireless bridge then ties the group of wired devices into your wireless network.

**Figure 4-12**   A Wireless Ethernet Bridge Allows Wired Devices to Connect to Your Wireless Home Network

# What Went Wrong: Your Quick Fix Reference

Before you set out to the store with your shopping list, be sure to take a quick look at some things you'll need to watch out for:

- If you're going to install a wireless network, remember that 802.11a is incompatible with both 802.11b and 802.11g. You can mix 802.11b and 802.11g equipment, but you'll lose the 802.11g performance advantage.

- Access points don't offer the firewall protection that you find in routers. Choosing an access point rather than a router for the interface between your home network and the Internet is asking for trouble because hackers will be able to access your network.

- Poor-quality cables can prevent your wired network from performing properly. Make sure you look for Cat5E cables to avoid problems.

- Mixing equipment brands on your wireless network means that you won't be able to take advantage of the Linksys SpeedBooster technology. Best practice is to choose a single standard for all the equipment.

# Summary

In this chapter, you learned about the specific equipment that you will need to set up your wired, wireless, or mixed home network. Armed with your shopping list, you should now be able to buy the correct set of equipment to completely set up your home network.

In the next chapter, you learn how to install your new networking equipment. Even if you've never opened up a computer, you'll see that the whole process is quite simple and easy.

# Things You'll Learn

- Installing network adapters in your PCs
- Choosing the correct location for your network hardware
- Adding the centerpiece of your home network

# Chapter 5

# Installing Your Network Hardware: This Won't Hurt a Bit

Now that you've done your shopping and have brought home the various bits and pieces of network hardware, it's time to install everything. This is the part of the project that seems most intimidating, but as you will soon find, it's not really difficult, and you might discover that installing the hardware is actually interesting.

## Installing Network Adapters: It's Easier Than You Think

You have now come to the point where you must install your network adapters (also known as network interface cards, or NICs). These are the only pieces of hardware that you will be installing that actually need to go inside your PC. If you're at all nervous about opening up your PC, it will be important for you to follow along carefully so that the process goes smoothly.

 **TIP** If you're really nervous about opening up your PC, try to find a friend or relative who has done so before to help you with the first one.

## PCI Network Adapters

A PCI network adapter must be installed inside your PC. The procedure that you follow is pretty much the same for both wired PCI network adapters as well as for wireless PCI network adapters. In both cases, you must physically install the adapter and the correct software drivers.

It's important to remember that the exact sequence of steps you will follow can vary depending on the version of Windows that your PC runs and on the type of network adapter you are installing. In some cases, you must install the drivers before you install the network adapter, whereas, in others, you install the network adapter first. Each Linksys network adapter (as well as network adapters from other vendors) includes a quick installation guide that specifies the correct order for your combination of Windows version and network card. In the following sections, you see each type of installation step by step.

Installing a PCI network adapter is the most complicated thing that you need to do to install your home network. If you have additional desktop PCs that require PCI network adapters, repeat the step-by-step procedures as necessary for each of them. When you have finished with that task, setting up the rest of your network will be very easy.

**Step-by-Step: Installing Drivers First**

If the quick installation guide directs you to install the drivers before you install the network adapter, follow these steps:

**Step 1.** Close any programs you might have open on your PC. You need to shut down your computer after you install the drivers, and closing any programs first can help avoid any conflicts.

**Step 2.** Insert the CD-ROM that came with the network adapter into your CD drive and wait for the setup wizard to start, as shown in Figure 5-1. If the setup wizard does not run automatically, check the quick installation guide for tips on how you can start it manually.

**Figure 5-1** The Start of the Setup Wizard

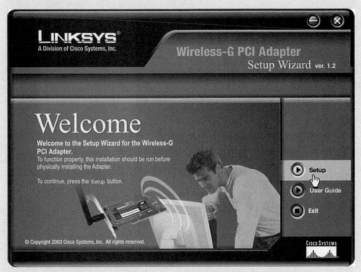

**Step 3.** Click the **Setup** button to continue.

**Step 4.** If a license agreement screen similar to Figure 5-2 is displayed, click the **Next** button to continue. In some cases, this screen might not appear, but if it does, you must accept the license agreement to continue the installation.

**Figure 5-2**    Accept the License Agreement to Continue

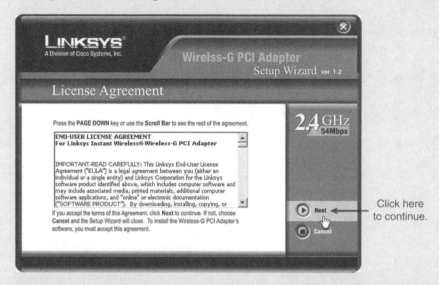

**Step 5.**    Because this example shows the installation of a wireless network adapter, you must next choose the network mode, as shown in Figure 5-3. In this case, choose the **Infrastructure Mode** option, because your network will include a wireless router.

**Figure 5-3**    Choose the Wireless Network Settings

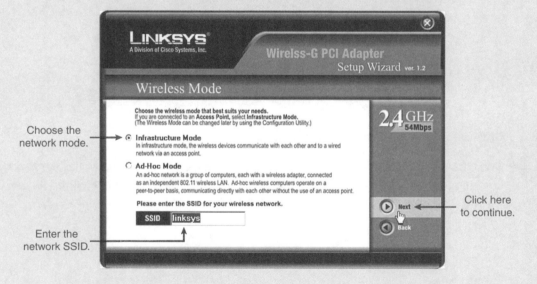

Step-by-Step: Installing Drivers First

**Step 6.** Enter the SSID for your router in the SSID box. For now, you can leave this set to linksys. Chapter 7, "Making Your Network Secure: Locking the Network's Door," explains what an SSID is and shows you how to set a more secure value for this option.

**Step 7.** Click the **Next** button to continue and display the Finalize Settings screen shown in Figure 5-4.

**Figure 5-4** Review the Wireless Network Settings

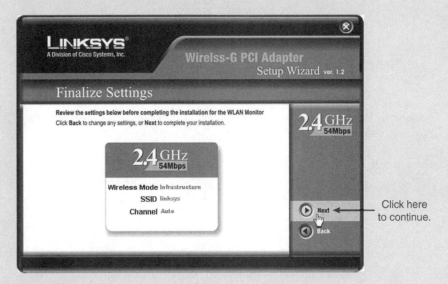

**Step 8.** Click **Next** to Continue.

**Step 9.** If you see a warning message telling you that a valid digital signature was not found, as shown in Figure 5-5, click **Yes** to continue. This message simply means that the driver hasn't been through Microsoft's certification procedure— not that anything is wrong with the driver.

**Figure 5-5**  Digital Signature Not Found: Click **Yes** to Continue

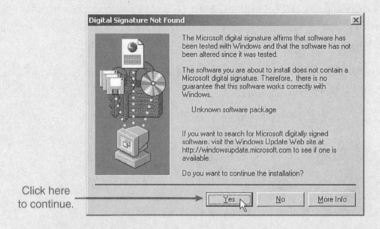

Click here
to continue.

**Step 10.** When the final Setup Wizard screen appears, as shown in Figure 5-6, click the **Exit** button to close the wizard.

**Figure 5-6**  The Setup Wizard Is Complete

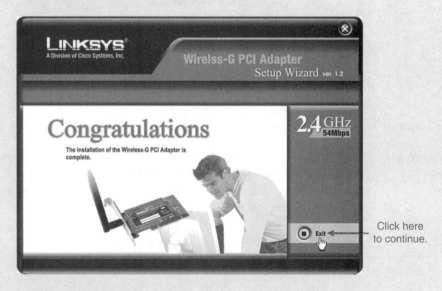

Click here
to continue.

**Step 11.** Click the Windows **Start** button and choose **Shut Down**, as shown in Figure 5-7. Depending on your version of Windows, your Start menu might look a little different than in Figure 5-7.

Step-by-Step: Installing Drivers First

**Figure 5-7**   Click **Start** and then **Shut Down**.

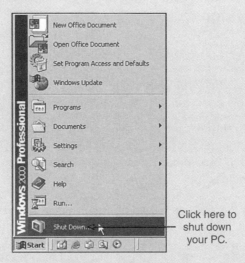

Click here to
shut down
your PC.

**Step 12.** Select the **Shut Down** option, as shown in Figure 5-8. Remember that this
might look a little different depending on your version of Windows, but you
still want to choose the option that turns off your PC.

**Figure 5-8**   Choose **Shut Down** and then **OK**.

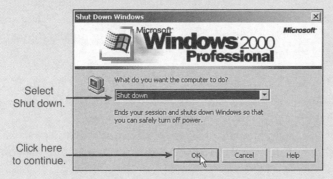

Select
Shut down.

Click here
to continue.

**Step 13.**   Click the **OK** button to turn off your PC.

At this point, you are ready to begin installing your network card into your desktop PC.

Step-by-Step: Installing Drivers First

## Step-by-Step: Installing Your PCI Network Adapter in Your Desktop PC

If you followed along the step-by-step procedure for installing drivers before installing the network adapter, your PC is already turned off. If your network adapter did not require you to install the drivers first, you should shut down your PC at this point. See Steps 11–13 in the previous step-by-step list if you need a little guidance on the proper way to do this.

This section takes you through the step-by-step procedure for installing a PCI network adapter inside a desktop PC. Be sure that you check the quick installation guide before proceeding to see if any preliminary steps—such as installing software drivers— must be completed before you install the adapter.

**Step 1.** With your PC already turned off, unplug the power cord from the back of the computer.

**Step 2.** Make note of where each of the cables plugs into the back of your PC. Many of the cables are color-coded, but you might find it useful to draw a picture of the back of your computer with a note showing where each cable connects. You can even use stickers on each cable to make it easier for you to reconnect the cables later.

**Step 3.** Carefully disconnect each of the cables from your PC. Most simply pull straight out, but a few—such as the one to your monitor—will probably be secured with two thumb screws or require pushing in a tab that holds it in place as with a telephone cable.

**Step 4.** If your system is a tower model (one of those tall units that typically stands on the floor under your desk), lay it down on its right side (as viewed from the front) so that the expansion slot covers are vertical, as shown in Figure 5-9. If your system normally sits on your desk under your monitor, it will already be in this position—but you need to move your monitor before continuing.

**Figure 5-9** Make Sure the Expansion Slot Covers Are in a Vertical Position

Expansion Slot Covers

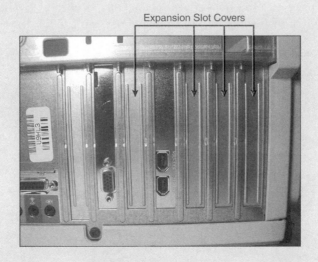

**Step 5.** Remove the cover from the side of your PC. This might require loosening a thumbscrew or releasing a latch or two and then sliding the cover slightly toward the rear. If you aren't sure how to remove the cover, don't worry; surprisingly, many people don't know how to do this! Simply consult your owner's manual to find out how to do this on your computer. After you remove the cover, you should see the expansion slots, as shown in Figure 5-10.

**Figure 5-10** Locate an Open PCI Expansion Slot

Expansion Slot Covers

Open PCI Expansion Slots

Installing Your PCI Network Adapter in Your Desktop PC

**Step 6.** Using a Phillips screwdriver, remove the screw that holds the cover for the expansion slot you want to use for the network adapter, as shown in Figure 5-11. Note that the covers for PCI slots are just to the left of their associated slots.

**Figure 5-11** Unscrew the Expansion Slot Cover

Remove the cover for the expansion slot you want to use.

**Step 7.** Lift out the cover, as shown in Figure 5-12.

**Figure 5-12** Remove the Expansion Slot Cover

**Step 8.** Carefully insert the network adapter into the open PCI expansion slot and push it straight down, as shown in Figure 5-13, until the card is fully seated in the slot. Both ends of the connector must be level in the slot and the bracket will be flush with the other brackets when the board is inserted properly.

**Figure 5-13** Carefully Push the Network Adapter Completely into the Slot

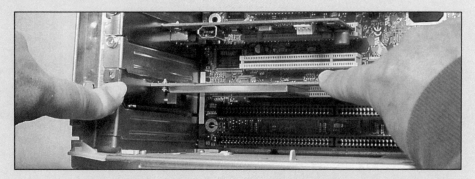

**Step 9.** Using the screw that held the expansion slot cover in place, fasten the network adapter, as shown in Figure 5-14.

**Figure 5-14** Fasten the Network Adapter into the Slot

Replace
the screw.

**Step 10.** Replace the cover on your PC.

**Step 11.** If you installed a wireless network adapter, such as the Linksys WMP54G, carefully screw on the antenna, as shown in Figure 5-15.

Installing Your PCI Network Adapter in Your Desktop PC

**Figure 5-15** Screw on the Antenna

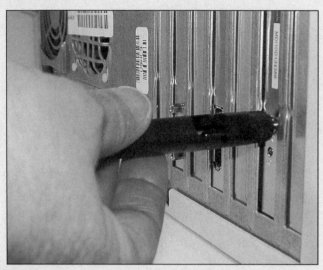

**Step 12.** Place your PC back into its normal position, and reconnect each of the cables you removed in Step 3.

Depending on the type of network adapter you are installing and the version of Windows on your PC, you might be finished at this point. If the quick installation guide instructs you to install the drivers after installing the network adapter, follow along with the next step-by-step procedure to install those drivers.

**Step-by-Step: Installing Drivers After Your Network Adapter Is Installed**

This section takes you through the step-by-step procedure for installing the software drivers after a PCI network adapter is installed inside a desktop PC. Be sure that you check the quick installation guide before proceeding to see if the drivers need to be installed before or after the hardware.

**Step 1.** Turn on the power and start your PC. Log in if you don't have an automatic login set up and wait for Windows to finish loading. Wait for the Found New Hardware Wizard to appear, as shown in Figure 5-16. Depending on your version of Windows, this wizard might have a slightly different appearance.

**Figure 5-16** The New Hardware Wizard Helps You Install Drivers

Click here
to continue.

**Step 2.** Click **Next** to continue and display the choices shown in Figure 5-17.

**Figure 5-17** Choose the Option to Search for the Drivers

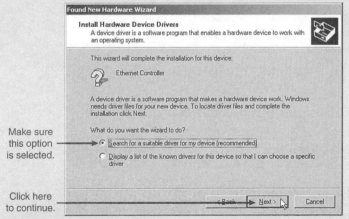

Make sure
this option
is selected.

Click here
to continue.

**Step 3.** Select the **Search for a suitable driver for my device** option to search for the drivers, and click **Next** to continue and display the options shown in Figure 5-18.

**Figure 5-18** Choose the Specify a Location Option

Select the option to specify a location.

Click here to continue.

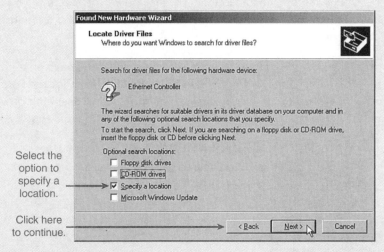

**Step 4.** Remove the check from all the options except the Specify a location option, and then click **Next** to continue.

**Step 5.** Insert the CD-ROM that came with your network adapter. If the setup wizard appears, click **Cancel** or **Exit** (as appropriate) to close the setup wizard and return to the New Hardware Wizard.

**Step 6.** Specify the correct location for the drivers, as shown in Figure 5-19. This location is specified in the quick installation guide and might vary depending on your version of Windows. You can click the **Browse** button to locate the correct folder.

**Figure 5-19** Specify the Location for the Driver

Click here to continue.

Specify the correct location.

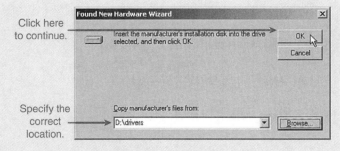

**Step 7.** When the wizard indicates that it has found the driver, as shown in Figure 5-20, ·click **Next** to continue and install the driver.

**Figure 5-20** The Wizard Is Now Ready to Install the Driver

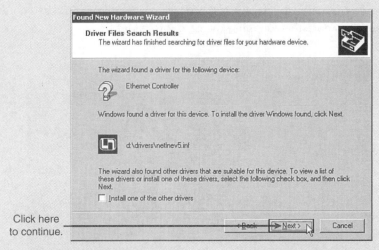

Click here
to continue.

**Step 8.** When you see a message like the one shown in Figure 5-21, the driver has been installed. Click the **Finish** button to close the wizard. Depending on your Windows version, you might have to restart Windows before you will be able to use the network adapter.

**Figure 5-21** The Drivers Have Been Installed Successfully

Click here
to finish.

Installing Drivers After Your Network Adapter Is Installed

# PC Card Network Adapters

Compared to installing a PCI network adapter in a desktop PC, installing a PC Card network adapter in a laptop is a piece of cake. You don't need to open your laptop to install a PC Card. In fact, as Figure 5-22 shows, the physical process of installing a PC Card network adapter requires nothing more than slipping the card into a slot that you'll find on one side of your laptop.

**Figure 5-22** Installing a PC Card Network Adapter

 **CAUTION** It is very important that you check the quick installation guide before you insert your PC Card network adapter. Otherwise, you might cause problems with the driver installation that can be very difficult to resolve.

The quick installation guide for the Linksys WPC54GS Wireless-G network adapter shown in Figure 5-22 instructs you to install the drivers before you insert the adapter into your laptop PC. To do so, you insert the CD-ROM into your CD drive and follow along as described in the section "Step-by-Step: Installing Drivers First" earlier in this chapter.

# USB Network Adapters

USB network adapter are also easy to install—either on a laptop or a desktop PC. As is the case with PC Card network adapters, USB network adapters simply plug into an open port on your PC. Figure 5-23 shows the Linksys WUSB54G Wireless-G USB network adapter plugged into a laptop PC.

**Figure 5-23** A USB Network Adapter

Each Linksys USB network adapter also includes a quick installation guide that will tell you if the drivers for the network adapter should be installed before or after you first insert the adapter into your PC. Remember that the procedure might vary depending on the version of Windows on each PC, so it's possible that some of the PCs on your home network will require a different procedure than your other PCs. The important thing to remember is that taking your time and doing the driver installation correctly will save you a lot of time in the end.

# Adding a Switch, a Router, or an Access Point: The Center of Your Network

Now that your network adapters are installed, you are ready to install the centerpiece of your network. For most home networks, this will be a router—either wired or wireless, depending on your choice of network types. If your network does not share an Internet connection, you might have decided to use a switch or a wireless access point, but that decision will have little impact on what you need to do next.

Your router (or other network centerpiece) has several requirements that affect your choice of its best location. Consider the following points in choosing where you will place your router:

- The router will need to be powered. Normally, this means that you must place it near an electrical outlet (unless you buy the Linksys WAPPOE Power Over Ethernet Adapter Kit—see Chapter 8, "Sharing Your Network," for more information on using the kit).

- Wired routers require a network cable that runs directly between the router and each PC or other networked device. This means you'll want to physically locate the router in an accessible and fairly central location.

- You cannot use the port on the router that is labeled Internet or WAN to connect to a PC.

- When plugging in the network cables, it's important to plug them in firmly until you hear a click.

- Network cables can be rather unsightly, so you might want to choose a router location that enables you to hide the cabling as much as possible.

- Wireless routers generally work best if they are mounted near the physical center of the network in a location that is as high as possible.

- Routers that are used for sharing an Internet connection must be connected to the Ethernet cable from the cable, DSL, or wireless modem using the port that is labeled Internet or WAN.

 **NOTE** In Chapter 8, you will learn about some additional types of locations for wireless networking equipment in the event that you want to share a wireless network over a longer distance.

After you have selected the proper location for your router, you simply unpack the router, connect the network cables, and connect the power. In Chapter 6, "Configuring Your Network: Bringing Everything Together," you learn how to do basic router configuration so that your home network will finally begin functioning.

# What Went Wrong: Your Quick Fix Reference

Installing network adapters is not difficult, but you need to watch out for a few potential trouble spots. Here are some things you might encounter and what to do if you have these problems:

- Network adapter drivers vary depending on the version of Windows that is in use. If you install a network adapter before its driver and find out that the driver needed to be installed first, open the Windows Control Panel and use the System icon to locate the network adapter. Right-click the adapter and choose Remove or Uninstall. Shut down your PC, remove the adapter, restart your computer, and then install the driver properly. Following this, shut down your computer and install the network adapter.

- If you rush in and just pull the cables off the back of your PC, it's quite easy to be confused when you go to hook everything up after you finish installing a network adapter. Don't panic. Most of the cables are either color-coded or will fit only one of the jacks. One handy thing to remember is that your speakers plug into the green jack.

- On some PCs, the expansion slot covers lack individual screws. If you open your PC but cannot see how to remove the expansion slot cover so that you can insert your PCI network adapter, look for a couple of thumbscrews on the back of the PC that are connected to a bracket that holds all the expansion slot covers in place. Loosening those thumbscrews allows the bracket to pivot so that you can remove the expansion slot cover and install the adapter.

- If your PC won't acknowledge that you installed the new PCI network adapter and you're certain that you followed the proper order for the physical installation and driver installation, the network adapter might not be fully seated in the slot. Shut down your PC, open the cover, remove the screw holding the adapter in place, and reseat the adapter. Remember that both ends of the board must be fully seated into the PCI slot for the adapter to function.

# Summary

In this chapter, you learned how to physically install your networking equipment. You learned that you must follow the proper order—which depends on your version of Windows—to make sure that the network adapter drivers are installed correctly.

In the next chapter, you will learn how to perform basic network configuration so that you can begin using your new home network.

# Things You'll Learn

- Configuring your PCs for network access
- Setting up your router
- Getting to the Internet through your home network

# Chapter 6

# Configuring Your Network: Bringing Everything Together

Your network is now nearly ready to use. You have your network adapters installed, your router in place, and the cables connected. In this chapter, you learn how to set up your PCs to access the network. This chapter also shows you how to configure your router so that you will be able to access the Internet via your shared connection.

## Setting Up Your PCs: Be a Matchmaker

Each PC on a network needs to be configured properly to access the network. Think of the setup process as something similar to getting the food ready before a party. This is not a difficult task, but you will find that the newer versions of Windows, such as Windows XP, make the whole process a lot easier than the earlier versions of Windows did.

### Using the Windows XP Network Setup Wizard

Windows XP includes a network setup wizard that can be used to create a network setup disk (a disk that configures those other PCs using the same wizard) for use on the Windows 98, Windows 98 Second Edition, Windows Millennium Edition, Windows XP Home Edition, or Windows XP Professional versions of Windows. This wizard is by far the easiest way to configure your home network automatically, so this is the method to use if any of your home PCs are running Windows XP. The wizard sets up the network protocols, network names, and all the other little details that are so important to making your network function. You might need 5 to 10 minutes to complete the wizard.

# Step-by-Step: Using the Network Setup Wizard

To use the Windows XP Network Setup Wizard, you must be logged in with administrator privileges—which you probably are already. When you are ready, follow these steps:

**Step 1.** Click the Windows **Start** button and choose **Control Panel**.

The Windows XP Control Panel can have two completely different appearances—depending on the choices you have made. The Classic view shows all Control Panel icons in a single screen, whereas the Category view groups the icons according to their purpose.

**Step 2.** If your Control Panel uses the Classic view, open the **Network Connections** icon to display the Network Connections dialog box, as shown in Figure 6-1. If your Control Panel uses the Category view, click the **Network and Internet Connections** icon to display a task list.

**Figure 6-1** The Network Connections Dialog Box

Click here
to start the
Network Setup
Wizard

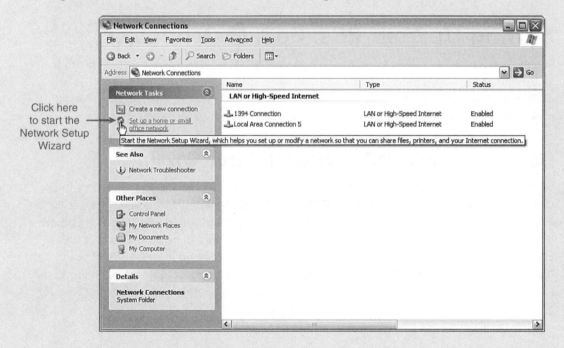

**Step 3.** Click the **Set up a home or small office network** link in the Network Connections dialog box or the **Set up or change your home or small office network** link in the Network and Internet Connections task list. In either case, this displays the Network Setup Wizard, as shown in Figure 6-2.

**Figure 6-2** Starting the Network Setup Wizard

Click here to continue.

**Step 4.** Click the **Next** button to continue and display the checklist shown in Figure 6-3.

**Figure 6-3** Verify That You Are Ready to Continue

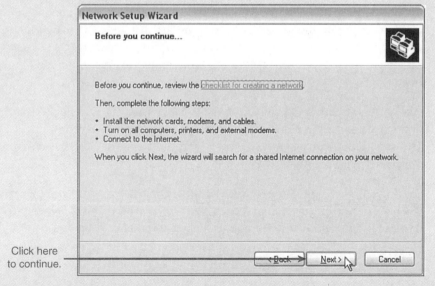

Click here to continue.

Step-by-Step: Using the Network Setup Wizard

**Step 5.** Click the **Next** button to continue. This displays the connection options shown in Figure 6-4.

**Figure 6-4** Choose Your Connection Method

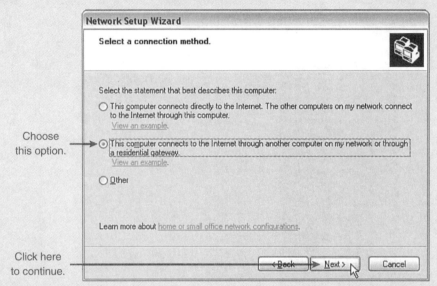

Choose this option.

Click here to continue.

**Step 6.** Because your home network connects through a router, choose the **This computer connects to the Internet through another computer on my network or through a residential gateway** option. You would select the first option if you did not have a router and wanted to make your Internet connection directly through the PC you are currently setting up. The third option, **Other**, is used primarily if you don't have an Internet connection or if you are setting up the network software before installing the network hardware. This book does not cover the first or third options because the second option is the most appropriate for the type of network recommended in this book.

**Step 7.** Click the **Next** button to continue. This typically displays the multiple connection options, as shown in Figure 6-5. If this screen is not shown, skip to Step 9. The screen appears only if you have more than one device that Windows considers to be a network adapter.

**Step 8.** Leave the first option, **Determine the appropriate connections for me (Recommended)**, selected and click **Next** to continue. This displays the Computer description and Computer name screen shown in Figure 6-6.

**Figure 6-5** Allow the Wizard to Choose the Connection

Choose
this option.

Click here
to continue.

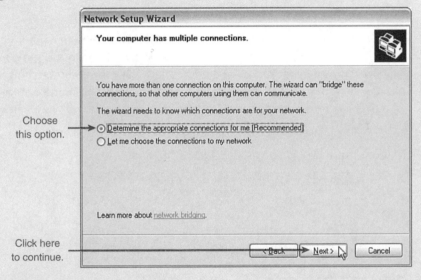

**Figure 6-6** Enter a Unique Name and Description

Enter a
name and
description.

Click here
to continue.

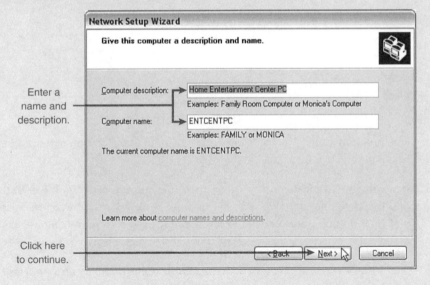

**Step 9.** Enter a description and a name for the PC you are configuring. The name must be unique on your network and should be no more than 15 characters (but without spaces or special characters, such as dollar signs). The names identify the different PCs on your network. The descriptions help further identify the different PCs if someone cannot do so from the name alone.

Step-by-Step: Using the Network Setup Wizard

**Step 10.** Click the **Next** button to continue and display the Workgroup name screen, as shown in Figure 6-7.

**Step 11.** Enter a name for your network (replacing the MSHOME entry that automatically appears). Every computer on your home network must be in the same workgroup to communicate. You need a name that's easy to remember and that uniquely identifies your network. Changing the workgroup name also makes it just a little bit harder for someone else to connect to your network without your permission.

**Figure 6-7**  Name Your Workgroup

Enter a workgroup name.

Click here to continue.

**Step 12.** Click the **Next** button to continue and display the verification screen, as shown in Figure 6-8.

**Step 13.** After you verify that the information shown is correct, click the **Next** button to continue. If you are connected to the Internet, your connection will be dropped briefly. Or if you spot an error, click the **Back** button to make any necessary corrections. When you continue, you see the screen shown in Figure 6-9.

**Step 14.** Choose the **Create a Network Setup Disk** option. This is an important step because you will later use this disk to run the Network Setup Wizard on your other PCs. You can also select the **Use my Windows XP CD** option and then use your Windows XP disc to run the wizard on your other PCs, but use caution to avoid starting the Windows XP installation wizard. If you already created a network setup disk, select the **Use the Network Setup Disk I already have** option or the **Just finish the wizard. I don't need to run the wizard on other computers** option.

**Figure 6-8**   Verify the Settings

Click here
to continue.

**Figure 6-9**   Create a Network Setup Disk

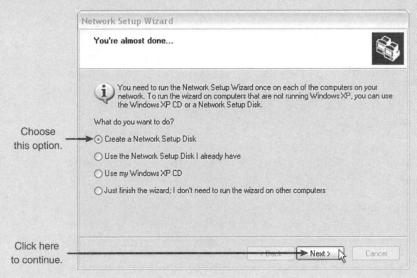

Choose
this option.

Click here
to continue.

**Step 15.** Click **Next** to continue. If you have more than one removable disk drive, you then see a screen similar to Figure 6-10. If you do not see this screen, skip to Step 17.

**Step 16.** Select **3 1/2 Floppy (A:)** and click **Next** to continue. This displays the screen shown in Figure 6-11. If you are using a different type of removable drive such as a USB key, select it instead of the floppy drive.

Step-by-Step: Using the Network Setup Wizard

**Figure 6-10** Choose the Drive to Create the Network Setup Disk

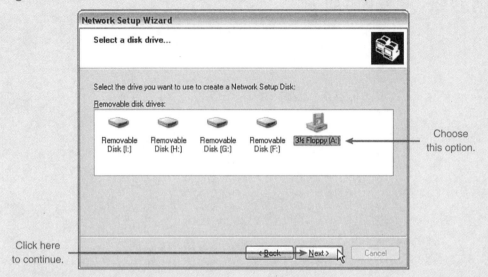

Choose this option.

Click here to continue.

**Figure 6-11** You Are Ready to Create the Network Setup Disk

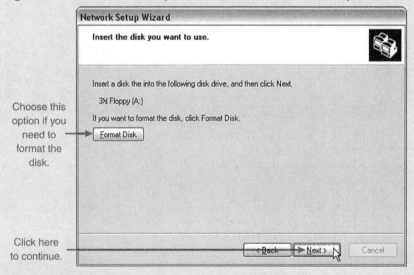

Choose this option if you need to format the disk.

Click here to continue.

**Step 17.** Insert your blank disk in drive A.

**Step 18.** If your disk must be formatted before it will be ready to use, click the **Format Disk** button and follow the prompts to format the disk. Otherwise, click **Next** to begin creating the Network Setup Disk.

**Step 19.** When the wizard is finished creating the Network Setup Disk, you see the screen shown in Figure 6-12. Click **Next** to continue.

HOME NETWORKING: A VISUAL DO-IT-YOURSELF GUIDE

**Figure 6-12** You Have Successfully Created the Network Setup Disk

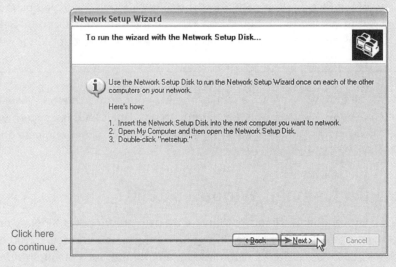

Click here
to continue.

**Step 20.** When the screen shown in Figure 6-13 appears, click the **Finish** button to close the Network Setup Wizard.

**Figure 6-13** You Have Successfully Completed the Network Setup Wizard

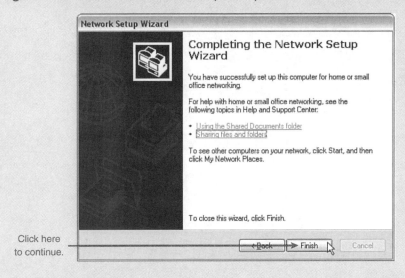

Click here
to continue.

**Step 21.** Remove the Network Setup Disk and repeat Steps 1–13 and 20 on each of the other PCs on your network.

**NOTE** If any of the PCs on your network is running Windows 2000, you cannot use the Network Setup Wizard to configure that PC. See the following section, "Setting Your PC's Name in Windows 2000," for information on how to set up Windows 2000.

You might think it strange to have to create a workgroup for your home network—especially if you intend to use your home network only for entertainment. Don't let this concern you. Having a workgroup is simply a method of allowing a group of PCs to communicate and is a necessary part of every Windows home network.

## Setting Your PC's Name in Windows 2000

Windows 2000 is the only version of Windows that cannot use the Windows XP Network Setup Wizard. Fortunately, this does not make setting up a PC running Windows 2000 difficult, because Windows 2000 was designed with networking in mind. As a result, Windows 2000 typically requires a little more than setting up the PC's name and workgroup to join your home network.

**Step-by-Step: Setting Your PC's Name in Windows 2000**

To set your computer's name and workgroup in Windows 2000, follow these steps:

**Step 1.** Click the Windows **Start** button and choose **Control Panel**.

**Step 2.** Open the **System** icon.

**Step 3.** Click the **Network Identification** tab, as shown in Figure 6-14.

**Figure 6-14** Open the Network Identification Tab of the System Properties Dialog Box

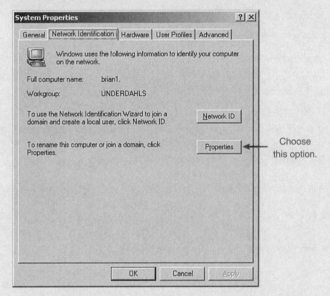

Choose this option.

**Step 4.** Click the **Properties** button to display the Identification Changes dialog box, as shown in Figure 6-15.

**Figure 6-15** Use the Identification Changes Dialog Box

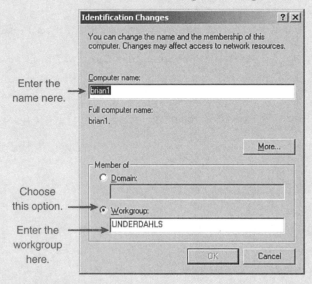

Enter the name nere.

Choose this option.

Enter the workgroup here.

**Step 5.** Enter a unique name for the PC in the Computer name text box.

**Step 6.** Make certain that the Workgroup option is selected.

**Step 7.** Enter the name of your home network's workgroup in the Workgroup text box.

**Step 8.** Click **OK** to close the Identification Changes dialog box.

**Step 9.** Click **OK** to close the System Properties dialog box.

# Setting Your PC's Name in Windows 98 or Windows Me

Even though the Windows XP Network Setup Wizard is the most convenient option for setting up your home network on Windows 98– or Windows Me–based PCs, you can use a similar procedure to the one required in Windows 2000 to set or change the PC's name on Windows 98 or Windows Me.

 **NOTE** If you're still using a PC that is running Windows 95, you might want to consider upgrading. Windows 95 tends to be rather difficult to set up for network use.

**Step-by-Step: Setting Your PC's Name in Windows 98 or Windows Me**

To set your computer's name and workgroup in Windows 98 or Windows Me, follow these steps:

**Step 1.** Click the Windows **Start** button and choose **Control Panel**.

**Step 2.** Open the **Network** icon.

**Step 3.** Click the **Identification** tab, as shown in Figure 6-16.

**Figure 6-16** Open the Identification Tab of the Network Dialog Box

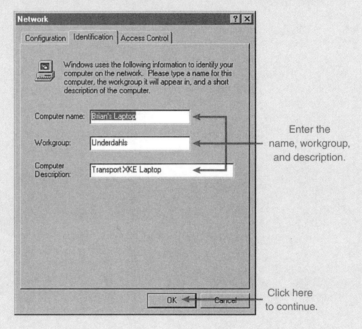

**Step 4.** Enter a unique name for the PC in the Computer name text box.

**Step 5.** Enter the name of your home network's workgroup in the Workgroup text box. Remember that all the PCs on your network must use the same workgroup name.

**Step 6.** Enter a description in the Computer Description text box.

**Step 7.** Click **OK** to close the Network dialog box.

Setting Your PC's Name in Windows 98 or Windows Me

TIP   Make sure that you have your Windows CD-ROM handy whenever you make changes to the network setup in Windows 98 or Windows Me. Both of these Windows versions tend to ask for the Windows disc regardless of how small any changes you've made are. You might even want to copy your Windows disc to your hard drive if you have the room so that you can avoid inserting the disc each time.

# Setting Up a Router/Gateway: Making the Internet Accessible

At this point, you are very close to the point where you can begin using your home network and allowing the PCs on your network to access the Internet. Next, you see how to access your router from your PC and do simple configuration tasks.

NOTE   The following section does not address the very important security issues that are involved in keeping your network safe. Be sure to read Chapter 7, "Making Your Network Secure: Locking the Network's Door," to learn more about this vital topic.

## Sorting Out the Internet Names

Your router acts both as the central point of your network and as the gateway between your network and the Internet. The router is able to sort out the traffic because each computer has its own, unique address. This address is known as an *IP address*—which is short for Internet Protocol address.

IP addresses are made up of a series of numbers that look like this (a series of four numbers separated by periods that range from 0 to 255):

   63.240.93.139

There is, however, one little problem with using IP addresses to surf the web: Who can possibly remember the IP addresses for all their favorite websites?

For example, open your web browser and enter the following address in the Address bar:

   **63.240.93.139**

After the page loads, it should be pretty clear that http://www.ciscopress.com would be easier to remember and far less error-prone, too. Fortunately, the Internet provides a service called Domain Name System (DNS) that translates names like http://www.ciscopress.com into IP addresses automatically.

In most cases, you don't need to worry about DNS because your Internet service provider (ISP) probably handles this detail automatically. Still, it's important to know that DNS exists because a few ISPs do require you to enter the IP addresses for the DNS servers manually. If they have told you to manually enter the DNS server addresses, you do so by configuring your router as described next.

## Finding Your Router on the Network

Even though DNS enables you to enter familiar-looking names to find your favorite websites, DNS is not available for the devices on your home network. To access the PCs, your router, or other devices on your home network, you have two options:

- The PCs can be accessed by name using Windows Explorer or Network Neighborhood by simply clicking the computer name.

- Any other device on the network can be accessed using an IP address in your web browser. You use an IP address to access the configuration options for your router, for example.

**Step-by-Step: Accessing Your Linksys Router**

To access your router so that you can view or modify its settings, follow these steps:

**Step 1.** Open your Web browser (such as Internet Explorer).

**Step 2.** Enter **192.168.1.1** in the address bar and click the **Go** button. This displays the Enter Network Password dialog box, as shown in Figure 6-17.

All Linksys routers use 192.168.1.1 as their default address.

**Figure 6-17** Use the Enter Network Password Dialog Box to Gain Access to Your Router

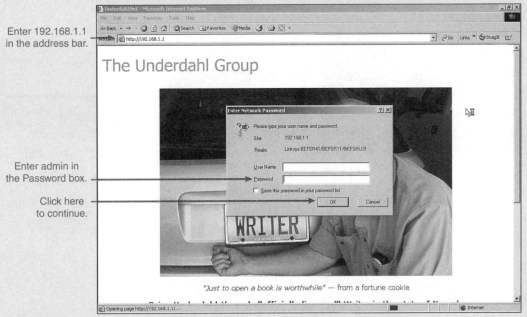

Enter 192.168.1.1 in the address bar.

Enter admin in the Password box.

Click here to continue.

**Step 3.** Enter **admin** in the Password text box. This must be lowercase. Leave the User Name text box blank.

All Linksys routers use admin as the default password.

**Step 4.** Click the **OK** button to continue. This displays the Linksys router configuration utility, as shown in Figure 6-18.

**Figure 6-18** The Setup Tab for Your Linksys Router

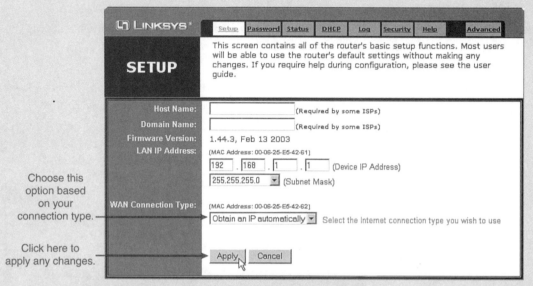

Choose this
option based
on your
connection type. —

Click here to
apply any changes. —

**Step 5.** Select the type of Internet connection from the drop-down list in the WAN Connection Type section. In most cases, the correct choice is the default Obtain an IP automatically.

**Step 6.** Click the **Apply** button if you have made any changes.

**Step 7.** Click the **DHCP** tab to view or modify the DHCP settings, as shown in Figure 6-19.

**Figure 6-19** The DHCP Tab for Your Linksys Router

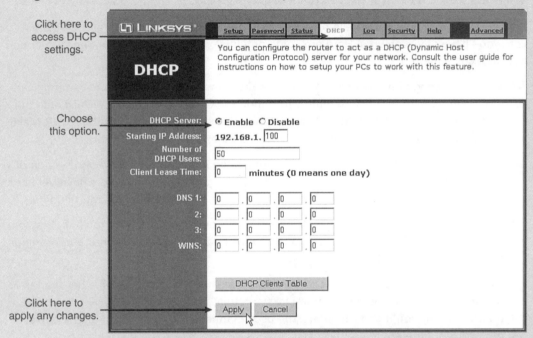

Click here to access DHCP settings.

Choose this option.

Click here to apply any changes.

**Step 8.** Make certain that the Enable option is selected. This allows your router to supply DHCP services to your network.

**Step 9.** Click the **Apply** button if you made any changes.

**Step 10.** Click the **Home** button in your browser's toolbar or enter the name of another website and click **Go** to close the router settings utility.

In Chapter 7, you will use the router settings utility to make additional changes to your router.

# What Went Wrong: Your Quick Fix Reference

Configuring your home network is pretty straightforward, but that doesn't guarantee that you won't have any problems. Here are some potential difficulties you might encounter and how to resolve them:

- All the PCs on your home network must use the same workgroup name to communicate easily with each other. By default, the Windows XP Network Setup Wizard sets the workgroup name to MSHOME whereas Windows 2000 defaults to WORKGROUP. Make sure that you have set the same workgroup name on each of your PCs.

- If you can see the other PCs on your network in the Network Neighborhood section of Windows Explorer but can't access those PCs, it might be that no folders have yet been shared. See Chapter 8, "Sharing Your Network," for information on sharing folders.

- If you cannot see the other PCs in Windows Explorer, you might need to configure your PC's firewall to add your network to a trusted zone. See Chapter 7 for more information on configuring firewalls.

- Even though all Linksys routers use 192.168.1.1 as their default address, other brands of routers might not. If you have a non-Linksys router, you can try 192.168.0.1 to access the router, but you'll need to check the user manual for details (such as the correct password or different IP addresses).

- Some ISPs require you to enter the IP address for the DNS server manually. If you find that you can access websites using IP addresses but not by using names, check to see if your ISP specifies DNS server addresses, and then enter them into the router configuration using the router setup utility.

- If you have a wireless network, each PC must use the same wireless security settings as your router to connect to the network. See Chapter 7 for more information on checking and modifying these settings if one or more of your PCs are unable to connect wirelessly.

# Summary

In this chapter, you learned how to configure the PCs on your network so that they can use the network to communicate. You saw that the Windows XP Network Setup Wizard makes short work of this task. You also learned how to change computer and workgroup names in earlier versions of Windows. Finally, you saw one example of how to connect a router for sharing Internet access.

In the next chapter, you learn how to make your network secure. A lot of dangers are out there just waiting to do damage, so it's vitally important for you to use the proper tools to keep your home network safe.

# Part III  Enhancing Your Network

This final part of the book shows you how to protect your home network from outside threats, how to share parts of the network with your family, and how to make entertainment a part of the network.

# Things You'll Learn

- Understanding the basics of network security
- Controlling access to your home network
- Preventing computer virus attacks

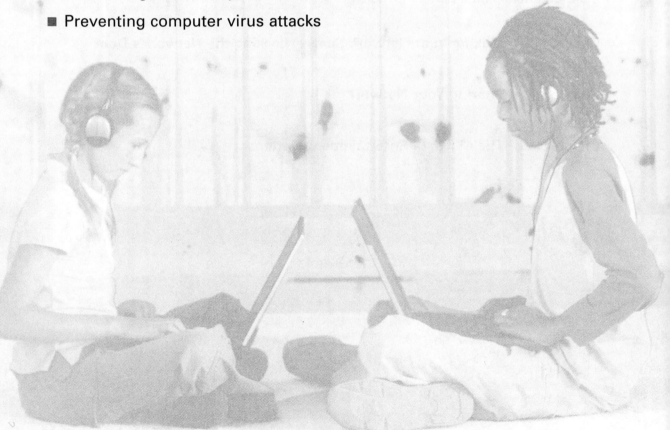

# Chapter 7

# Making Your Network Secure: Locking the Network's Door

It's unfortunate, but true—there are many threats to your network's safety and security. It will take a little work, but as this chapter will show you, it is possible to protect your network, your PCs, and your personal files from those threats. Ultimately, this chapter might end up being the most important one for you in this book.

## Understanding Security: You May Not Want It, but You Need It

You likely do a number of things to protect your personal property and security without giving those things very much thought. For example, you probably lock your doors, and you don't leave your car running in the parking lot when you go into the supermarket. Sure, these seem obvious, but that's because you recognize the dangers involved in not taking these precautions. Understanding the threats makes it much easier to visualize the necessary precautions to reduce or prevent those threats.

One problem with security threats to your home network is that it can be hard to understand just what those threats are. After all, have you ever thought, "No one would want to get into my computer because there's nothing for them to steal"? As long as you think like that, you do not understand how real the security problem really is. Consider the following list of just a few reasons why someone might want to gain access to your PCs:

- If you access your bank account or a credit card account by going online with your computer, your account numbers, user names, and passwords could be sitting there waiting for some thief to come along and clean out your account.

- If a spammer can gain control of your system, he could send out thousands of junk e-mails that appear to come from you. The result could be that your future real e-mail messages would be blocked or that your Internet account might be canceled.

- Hackers also like to take control of PCs so that they can launch coordinated attacks on websites from thousands of slave PCs at the same time. You can probably imagine how unpopular you would be with your Internet service provider (ISP) if your PC were one of the ones participating in one of these attacks.

- Computer virus writers sometimes create destructive code just to see if they can do it. They don't care if their virus wipes out years of hard work on your PCs. In fact, they'd probably be happy to know that it had happened. And you would definitely not be happy!

The list could go on, but you get the picture by now. The consequences of leaving your home network unsecured can be much worse than having your car stolen. It really doesn't matter how your PCs are used because the threats exist in any case. Connecting to the Internet simply makes you an easier target. You need to be concerned about safety and security if you're going to use a PC, and especially now that you have a home network that is likely connected to the Internet. You also need to be concerned about how easily someone can enter your wireless network from next door or even from the street in front of your house.

## Limiting Access: Closing the Barn Door Before the Cow Gets Out

Your first line of defense in virtually any situation is to control access to important resources. That's why banks keep their money in vaults rather than in bags by their front doors. If a customer comes in and needs cash, a trusted bank employee gains access to that vault and retrieves the currency. These types of strict controls ensure the safety and security of the bank's assets.

Likewise, controlling the access to your home network also helps protect your safety and security. You apply these controls using several types of security measures that are discussed in the sections that follow.

# Firewalls

In computer terms, a *firewall* is an application that controls the traffic between a network and the outside world—just as a firewall in a building is a wall constructed to stop the spread of fire. Routers often have basic hardware firewall functions built in, but for more complete and sophisticated protection, you need a software firewall running on your PCs.

Firewalls can be standalone programs that provide just firewall services, or they can be included in a more comprehensive program that has additional functions. Some examples of firewall programs include the following:

- ZoneAlarm from Zone Labs (http://www.zonelabs.com) is a basic firewall that you can download and use on your home PCs for free. The basic version of ZoneAlarm provides just firewall protection services.

- ZoneAlarm Pro, also from Zone Labs (www.zonelabs.com), adds features such as popup blocking, cookie controls, and automatic configuration options. ZoneAlarm Pro is available on an annual subscription basis, but you can try the program for free on a 30-day trial basis.

- Norton Personal Firewall from Symantec (http://www.symantec.com) is similar to ZoneAlarm Pro, but you might want to consider Symantec's more complete Norton Internet Security, which includes antivirus protection, an e-mail spam blocker, and parental controls (so that you can control your children's access to certain websites).

 **TIP**   Many Linksys routers include a 60-day trial version of Norton Internet Security in the package.

Windows XP has a very basic firewall called Internet Connection Firewall built-in. Although this basic firewall is better than nothing, it does not offer nearly as much protection as even the free version of ZoneAlarm. If you do not want to pay for one of the more comprehensive security packages, ZoneAlarm is a far better choice than relying upon the Windows XP Internet Connection Firewall.

Table 7-1 compares some of the important features of these products.

**Table 7-1**   Comparison of Firewall Products

| Feature | Windows XP Internet Connection Firewall | Norton Internet Security | Norton Personal Firewall | Norton Antivirus | ZoneAlarm | ZoneAlarm Pro |
|---|---|---|---|---|---|---|
| Antivirus | | Yes | | Yes | | |
| Antispam | | Yes | | | | |
| Parental Control | | Yes | | | | |
| Privacy Control | | Yes | Yes | | | Yes |
| Firewall | Yes (limited) | Yes | Yes | | Yes | Yes |
| E-mail Protection | | Yes | | Yes | Yes | Yes |
| Ad Blocking | | Yes | | | | Yes |

Zone Labs now also offer a version of ZoneAlarm which includes antivirus protection.
See http://www.zonelabs.com for more information.

## Allowing and Restricting Outside Access

Because a firewall is designed to control access, it restricts the capability of other computers to connect to your PC. A good firewall also controls the capability of programs that are running on your PC to connect to the outside world. These types of restrictions help keep your computer safe, but they also complicate the whole process of networking because the PCs on your home network do need access to each other if they are going to share files or other resources. In this section, you learn how to configure the ZoneAlarm firewall to make your network usable.

**Step-by-Step: Configuring a Firewall for Network Access**

Before following along with this procedure, you should download and install ZoneAlarm on your PC. If you are using a different firewall product, the steps will be similar but not identical.

 **TIP** Each PC on your home network will need to be configured, as shown in the following step-by-step procedure.

To configure ZoneAlarm to enable local network access, follow these steps:

**Step 1.** Click the Windows **Start** button and **Programs > Zone Labs > Zone Labs Security** to display the ZoneAlarm window, as shown in Figure 7-1.

**Figure 7-1** The ZoneAlarm Main Window

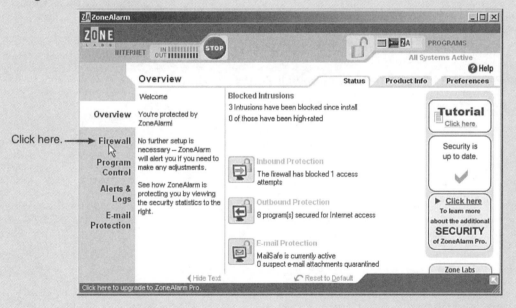

**Step 2.** Click the word **Firewall** on the left side of the window to display the firewall settings, as shown in Figure 7-2.

**Step 3.** Click the **Zones** tab in the upper-right area of the Firewall Settings window. This displays the ZoneAlarm Firewall Zones window, as shown in Figure 7-3.

Configuring a Firewall for Network Access

**Figure 7-2** The ZoneAlarm Firewall Settings Window

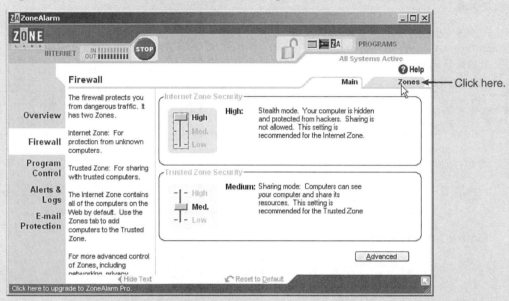

Click here.

**Figure 7-3** The ZoneAlarm Firewall Zones Window

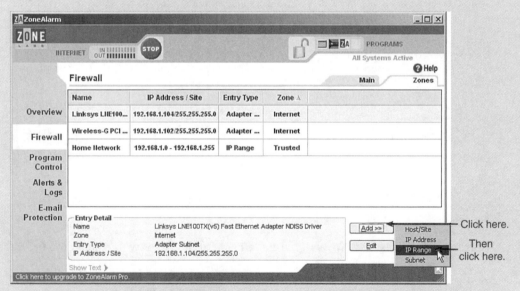

Click here.

Then click here.

**Step 4.** Click the **Add** button to display the popup menu shown in the lower-right section of Figure 7-3.

**Step 5.** Click **IP Range** on the menu to display the Add IP Range dialog box, shown in Figure 7-4.

**Figure 7-4**   The Add IP Range Dialog Box

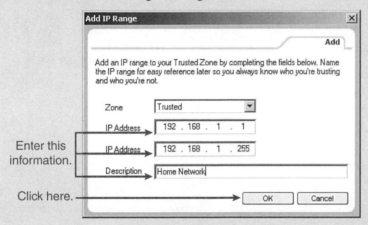

**Step 6.** Make certain that Trusted is selected in the drop-down Zone list box. This is the default setting and it enables you to add the IP address range for your home network to the trusted zone.

**Step 7.** Enter **192.168.1.1** in the upper IP Address box. This establishes the start of the address range you will add. It is appropriate for the default configuration for all Linksys networking equipment.

**Step 8.** Enter **192.168.1.255** in the lower IP Address box. This establishes the end of the address range you will add. This range enables you to add as many PCs as you like to your home network without the necessity of making further modifications.

**Step 9.** Enter a name for this range of addresses in the Description text box. Use a name like **Home Network** that is easy for you to remember.

Configuring a Firewall for Network Access

**Step 10.** Click the **OK** button to continue and to close the Add IP Range dialog box.

**Step 11.** Click the **Apply** button, as shown in Figure 7-5.

**Figure 7-5** Apply Your Changes

**Step 12.** Click the **Close** (X) button in the upper-right corner of the ZoneAlarm window. If you see a message informing you that this will not exit the program, click **OK** to confirm. You want the ZoneAlarm program to remain running in the Windows System Tray.

By adding the range of IP addresses between 192.168.1.1 and 192.168.1.255 to the trusted zone, you enable devices within that range to communicate freely without being blocked by the firewall. Because this range of IP addresses cannot be accessed from outside of your network, it is safe to trust this range. The exact IP address range you need to use will vary if you're using a non-Linksys router or using a Linksys router that was set up using something other than the default configuration. Consult your product documentation for details.

## Online Games and Your Firewall

Many types of programs need Internet access to function properly. Online games are one such example, of course. There's just one little problem, though, and that is your firewall. The primary function of a firewall is to control traffic, and this means that the firewall can block programs like games from getting the Internet access they need.

The solution is to configure your firewall so that it allows Internet access to those programs that have a legitimate reason to use the Internet. In this section, you learn how to configure the program control features of your firewall so that your online games will function properly.

# Step-by-Step: Configuring a Firewall's Program Control

As with the previous step-by-step procedure, configuring a firewall's program control uses ZoneAlarm to illustrate the process. Other firewall products will be similar but not identical.

To configure the program control feature in ZoneAlarm, follow these steps:

**Step 1.** Click the Windows **Start** button and **Programs > Zone Labs > Zone Labs Security** to display the ZoneAlarm window.

**Step 2.** Click **Program Control** along the left side of the ZoneAlarm window to display the Program Control tab, as shown in Figure 7-6.

**Figure 7-6** The ZoneAlarm Program Control Tab

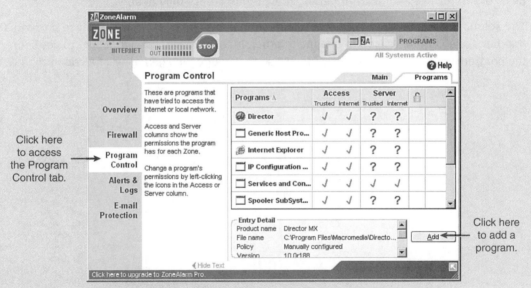

**Step 3.** Click the **Add** button in the lower-right corner of the ZoneAlarm window to display the Add Program dialog box, as shown in Figure 7-7.

**Step 4.** Use the drop-down **Look in** box to navigate to the folder that contains the program you want to add to the program control list. Note that ZoneAlarm automatically opens the Add Program dialog box in the Program Files folder, so you should be able to locate the program folder fairly easily.

**Step 5.** Click the icon for the program you want to add.

**Step 6.** Click the **Open** button to close the Add Program dialog box and return to the ZoneAlarm window. As Figure 7-8 shows, the new program will now appear in the list on the Program Control tab.

**Figure 7-7** The Add Program Dialog Box

Navigate to the
program folder.

Select the
program.

Click here
to continue.

**Figure 7-8** Your New Program Is Now Listed

Click here to set
the program's
access permissions.

Select Allow from
the pop-up menu.

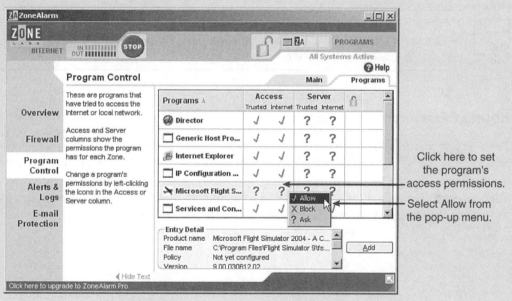

**Step 7.** Click the question mark (?) in the Internet column under Access of the program's row to pop up the menu shown in Figure 7-8.

**Step 8.** Click **Allow** to allow the program to access the Internet. This also allows the program to access the Trusted zone.

**Step 9.** Repeat Steps 3 through 8 for any additional programs you want to allow to access the Internet.

You can also allow programs to access the Internet by clicking Yes when ZoneAlarm pops up a message window at the lower-right of your monitor asking if you want to allow the program to access the Internet. For most types of programs, clicking Yes in the popup is easier than manually adding the program, as shown in the preceding step-by-step procedure. Games, however, might prevent the popup from appearing, so the manual procedure is a sure-fire way to configure the access.

## Wireless Network Security

A firewall does a very good job of protecting your network in most instances; however, if you have a wireless network, you need to take some additional steps to keep your network secure. The same thing that makes a wireless network so convenient—the fact that you don't have to run wires to each PC—is also the thing that makes these extra steps so important. Because you can't physically prevent someone else from connecting to your wireless network, you need to take some extra precautions to electronically prevent people from doing so.

---

 **TIP**   You might want to apply each security setting one at a time and test the results before proceeding. That way you will have an easier time correcting the problem if something goes wrong.

---

### Router Passwords

The first and possibly most important thing you should do to protect your wireless network is to change the default password. All Linksys routers use **admin** as the default password. If you do not change this, anyone within wireless range would be able to take control of your network. The default passwords for Linksys (and all other popular brands of routers) are well-known to attackers. In fact, they're posted on the Internet.

## Step-by-Step: Changing Your Wireless Router's Password

To change the password on your wireless router, follow these steps:

**Step 1.** Open your web browser, enter **192.168.1.1** in the address box, and click **Go** to display the Enter Network Password dialog box, as shown in Figure 7-9.

**Figure 7-9** Access Your Wireless Router Using Your Web Browser

**Step 2.** Enter **admin** in the Password text box. Make sure you have left the User Name box empty.

**Step 3.** Click **OK** to continue and display the setup utility as, shown in Figure 7-10.

**Figure 7-10** Click **Administration** to Access the Password

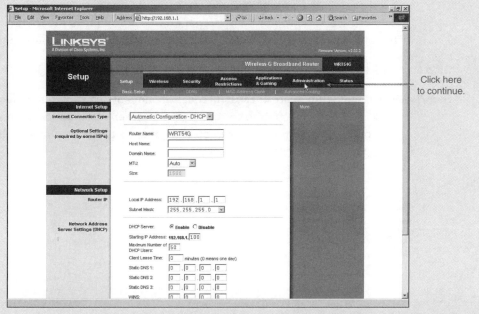

Step-by-Step: Changing Your Wireless Router's Password

**Step 4.**   Click **Administration** to access the Router Password screen shown in Figure 7-11.

**Figure 7-11** Set Your New Password

Enter and confirm your new password.

Click here to apply your changes.

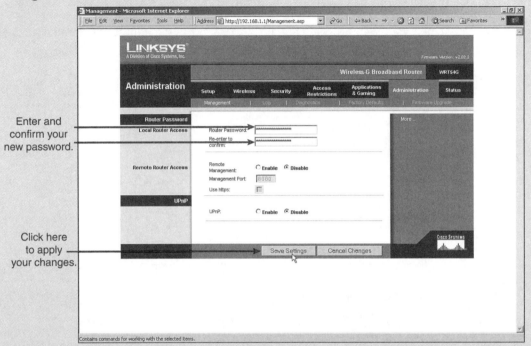

**Step 5.**   Enter your new password in the Router Password and Re-enter to confirm text boxes. Make certain that you remember the new password because you cannot access the router if you forget it (unless you press the router's Reset button—which will require you to completely reconfigure the router afterward).

**Step 6.**   Click the **Save Settings** button to save the new password.

**Step 7.**   When the Settings are successful message appears as shown in Figure 7-12, click the **Continue** button to return to the router setup utility. Do not close the router setup utility because you will continue to use it to make additional changes in the sections that follow.

Step-by-Step: Changing Your Wireless Router's Password

**Figure 7-12** Click **Continue** to Return to the Router Setup Utility

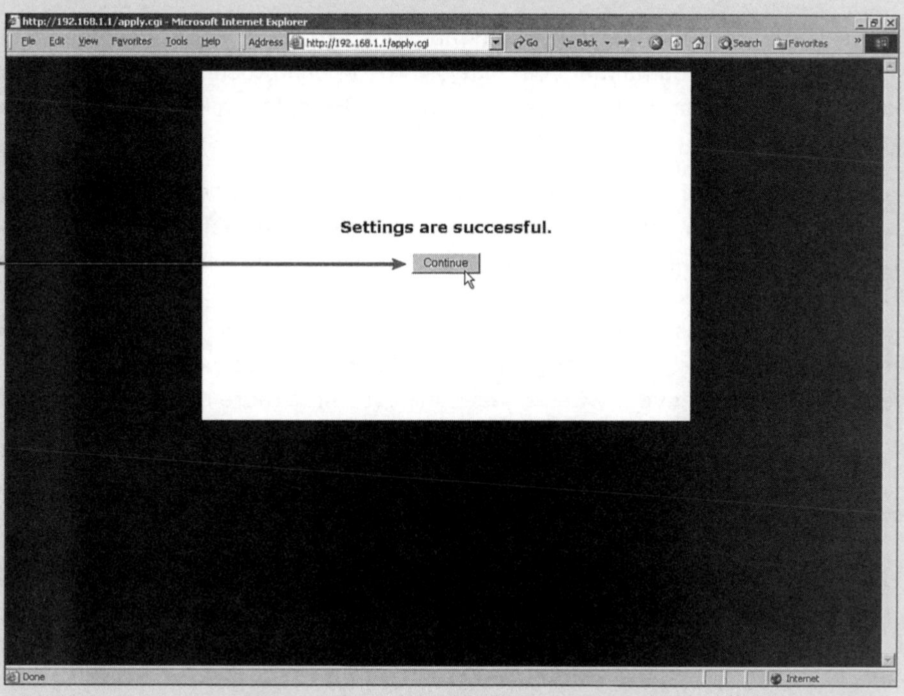

Click here
to continue.

Settings are successful.

Continue

## SSID (Network Name) Broadcasts

The next important change you should make is to the SSID (service set identifier) broadcasts. The SSID is a name that your wireless router can broadcast to make it easier for wireless devices to find and connect to your network. Here, too, all Linksys wireless routers are set to broadcast their default SSID—linksys.

Although broadcasting the SSID makes it easier for wireless devices to find your network, it's important to remember that you can't control who can see that broadcast. By broadcasting the SSID, you are, in effect, announcing to anyone who has a wireless adapter in their PC that your network is sitting there (and probably easy to access). In reality, you can easily configure the devices on your network to connect to a specific SSID without broadcasting the SSID from your router. Changing the SSID and stopping its broadcast are two important steps toward keeping your wireless network just a little more private.

**Step-by-Step: Changing Your Router's SSID Broadcast Settings**

To change the SSID broadcast setting on your wireless router, follow these steps:

**Step 1.** If the router setup utility is not still open from when you changed the router password, follow Steps 1–3 in the "Changing Your Wireless Router's Password" step-by-step procedure.

**Step 2.** Click the **Wireless** tab to display the settings shown in Figure 7-13.

**Figure 7-13** Modifying the SSID Settings

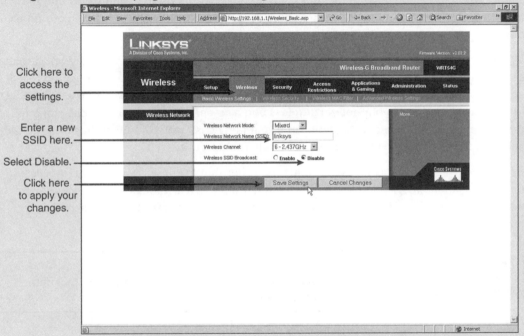

**Step 3.** Enter a new name for your router in the Wireless Network Name (SSID) text box. Security experts generally suggest using a name that does not easily identify you, such as your family name or address.

Remember that you also need to reconfigure the wireless network adapters in each of your PCs to use the new SSID.

**Step 4.** Select the **Disable** option to prevent the broadcast of the SSID.

**Step 5.** Click the **Save Settings** button.

**Step 6.** Click the **Continue** button to return to the router setup utility.

**NOTE**  In most cases, you should leave the Wireless Network Mode setting as Mixed to enable both 802.11b and 802.11g devices to connect. You might want to choose a different Wireless Channel setting in the event that you experience poor network performance that you think might be caused by interference, but normally you can simply leave this option alone.

## MAC Address Filtering

Earlier in this chapter in the "Configuring a Firewall for Network Access" step-by-step procedure, you learned how to set up your firewall to place a range of IP addresses into the trusted zone. This allows any PC with an IP address within that range to access your home network.

Unfortunately, opening up a range of IP addresses for access to your home network carries some risk if your network happens to be a wireless network. That's because opening this IP address range also allows other people to gain access if they have selected the correct SSID and are within range of your network (unless you also enable encryption, as described in the next section). It turns out that you can take a fairly easy step to prevent this undesirable situation from compromising your wireless network's security.

Each network adapter has its own unique identifier that is known as its Media Access Control (MAC) address. You can use this identifier to limit which devices can access your wireless network. The MAC address is typically printed on a sticker that is attached to each device.

 **NOTE**  It's possible for someone to change the MAC and thereby bypass MAC filtering, but you're going to have a hard time keeping someone who is that determined from attacking your network no matter what you do.

## Step-by-Step: Applying MAC Filtering on Your Wireless Router

To apply MAC filtering on your wireless router, first make sure that all the wireless devices on your network are turned on, and then follow these steps:

**Step 1.** If the router setup utility is not still open from the previous exercise, follow Steps 1 through 3 in the "Changing Your Wireless Router's Password" step-by-step procedure.

**Step 2.** Click the Wireless tab and then the Wireless MAC Filter selection to display the settings shown in Figure 7-14.

**Figure 7-14** Modifying the MAC Filtering Settings

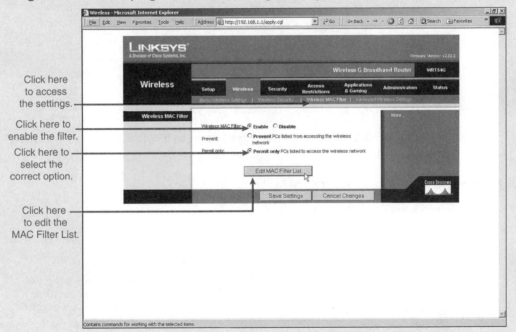

**Step 3.** Select the **Enable** option.

**Step 4.** Select the **Permit Only** option; this appears after you click **Enable**.

**Step 5.** Click the **Edit MAC Filter List** button to display the MAC Address Filter List, as shown in Figure 7-15.

**Figure 7-15** The MAC Filter List

Click here to access the list of wireless adapters.

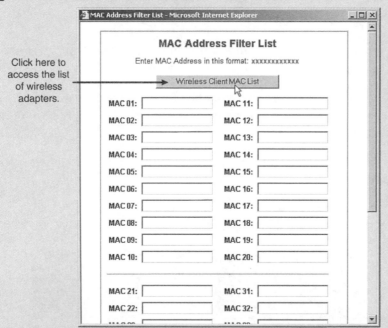

Step 6. Click the **Wireless Client MAC List** button to display the list, as shown in Figure 7-16.

**Figure 7-16** The Wireless Client MAC List

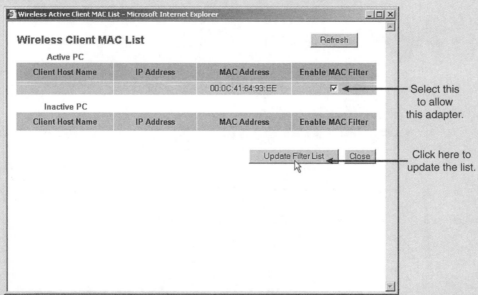

Select this to allow this adapter.

Click here to update the list.

Applying MAC Filtering on Your Wireless Router

**Step 7.** Select the **Enable MAC Filter** checkbox for each of the listed items.

**Step 8.** Click the **Update Filter List** button and return to the MAC Filter List window.

**Step 9.** Scroll to the bottom of the window in Figure 7-17 and click the **Save Settings** button.

**Figure 7-17** Scroll Down and Save Your Changes

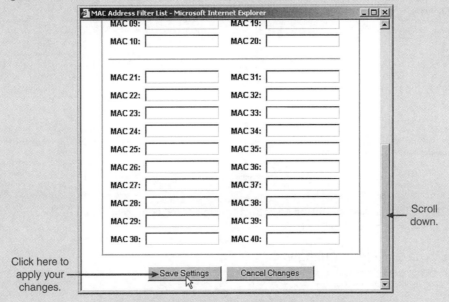

**Step 10.** When the "Settings are successful" message appears, as shown in Figure 7-18, click **Continue**.

Applying MAC Filtering on Your Wireless Router

**Figure 7-18** Settings Are Successful

Click here to apply your changes.

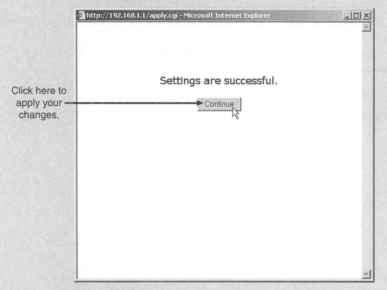

**Step 11.** Click the **Close** button to return to the router settings utility, as shown in Figure 7-19.

**Figure 7-19** Save Your Changes

Click here to apply your changes.

**Step 12.** Click the **Save Settings** button and then the **Continue** button.

Applying MAC Filtering on Your Wireless Router

## WEP Keys

The security modifications you have made so far will keep most casual PC users from easily accessing your wireless home network, but you should still take another step to make life difficult for more dedicated snoopers. That step is to apply encryption to the wireless signals.

 **NOTE**   You can use several types of encryption on your wireless network. This section focuses on Wired Equivalent Privacy (WEP) because even though Wi-Fi Protected Access (WPA) is considered to be more secure, WEP is still supported by more devices than is WPA. If all the equipment on your wireless network supports WPA, you should probably choose that option instead of WEP.

## Step-by-Step: Applying Encryption to Your Wireless Network

To apply WEP encryption on your wireless network, follow these steps:

**Step 1.** If the router setup utility is not still open from the previous exercise, follow Steps 1 through 3 in the "Changing Your Wireless Router's Password" step-by-step procedure.

**Step 2.** Click the **Wireless** tab and then the **Wireless Security** selection to display the settings shown in Figure 7-20.

**Figure 7-20** Modifying the Wireless Security Settings

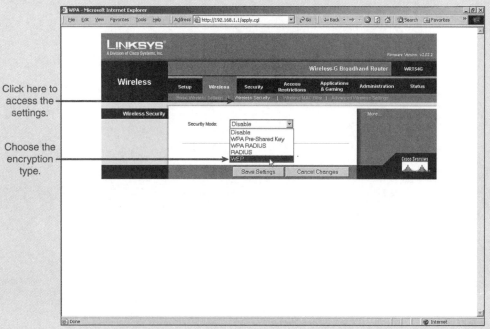

**Step 3.** Select the WEP option from the drop-down Security Mode list box. This will display additional choices, as shown in Figure 7-21.

**Step 4.** Select the **128 bits 26 hex digits** option from the WEP Encryption list box. This provides much better security than the default 64 bits 10 hex digits option.

**Step 5.** Enter a phrase in the Passphrase text box, as shown in Figure 7-22. The router settings utility will create WEP keys using this entry.

**Figure 7-21** Select the Highest Level of Encryption

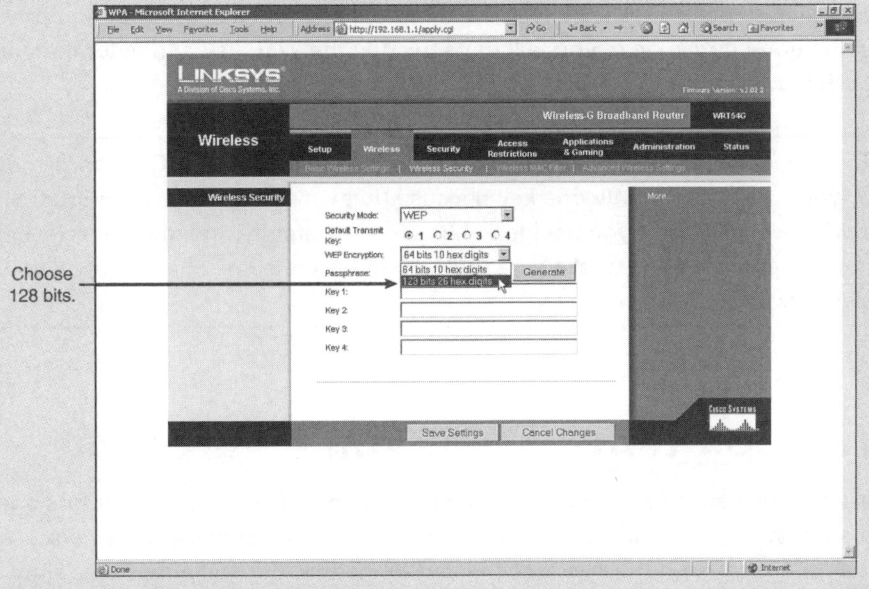

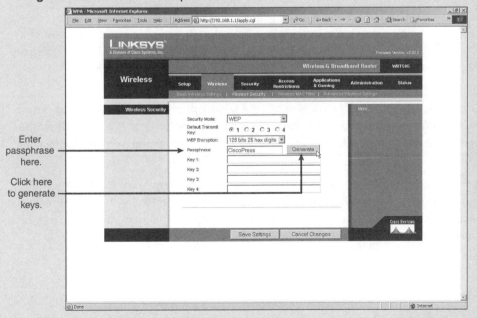

Choose
128 bits.

**Figure 7-22** Enter a Passphrase

Enter
passphrase
here.

Click here
to generate
keys.

**Step 6.** Click the **Generate** button to create the keys.

**Step 7.** Click the **Save Settings** button and then the **Continue** button.

Applying Encryption to Your Wireless Network

If all the wireless equipment on your network is from Linksys, you can use the same passphrase to generate the WEP keys using the setup utilities for each piece of equipment. If you have some non-Linksys gear, you will have to copy the WEP key and enter it manually to allow that other equipment to connect to your wireless network.

 **NOTE**   WEP allows you to set up four different encryption keys. On a home network, you typically use only one key because that way it's easier to configure all your wireless devices. If you decide to change the Default Transmit Key selection to any key other than Key 1, make sure that you make the same change on all your wireless devices.

# Antivirus Solutions: This Won't Hurt a Bit

Computer viruses aren't specifically a network-related issue, but protecting your PCs against the latest virus threats is just as important as any of the other security measures discussed in this chapter. An unprotected PC that is connected to the Internet will almost certainly become infected with a virus sooner or later, and the results can be staggering. In some cases, viruses have been able to wipe out every file on a computer, making the data impossible to recover and the PC useless without many hours of restoration.

Antivirus software helps protect your computers from the effects of computer viruses (and the closely related worms and Trojans). But antivirus software is effective only if it is actually installed on your PC and frequently updated so that new viruses can be detected.

 **CAUTION**   Antivirus software is sold on a subscription basis. If you do not renew the subscription when your coverage expires, you will be unable to download the latest virus definitions, and your computers will not be protected from virus infections.

The installation disc for Linksys routers includes a 60-day trial version of Norton Internet Security from Symantec (http://www.symantec.com), as shown in Figure 7-23. Norton Internet Security incorporates a number of very useful features including antivirus, personal firewall, antispam software, and website filtering.

**Figure 7-23** Click to Install Norton Internet Security

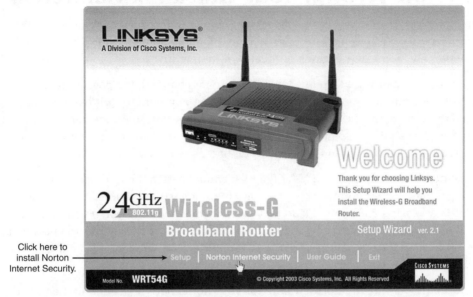

Click here to install Norton Internet Security.

You can also buy single-function programs such as Norton AntiVirus if you don't need all the features that are included in Norton Internet Security. No matter which antivirus software you buy, be sure to download updates at least once a week to maintain your protection.

**TIP**   Antivirus software typically does not protect you from another type of threat known as spyware. One of the most popular tools for fighting spyware is Ad-aware, which you can download from the Lavasoft website at http://www.lavasoft.nu.

# What Went Wrong: Your Quick Fix Reference

Maintaining the security of your home network can be one of the most complicated tasks in the entire procedure of setting up your own network. Here are some potential pitfalls you might encounter and some suggestions for dealing with them:

- If you attempt to follow the step-by-step procedure for changing the password on your wireless router but are unable to access your router, someone might have already changed the password. The solution is to press the Reset button on the back of your router to restore all default settings. Remember, though, that this means you will have to also reset every other setting you have modified on your router.

- The total number of items on the MAC filter list should match the number of wireless devices you have on your network. If there are more items than there should be, someone else is accessing your network. In that case, disable one device at a time and check to see if all your devices can still connect. It will take some work, but you will be able to remove the unauthorized device from the MAC filter list and prevent it from accessing your network.

- If you forget to add the IP address range for your home network to the trusted zone, your computers will be able to browse the Internet, but they won't be able to access anything on your home network. Adding an incorrect IP address range can also cause this effect, so if you encounter this type of problem, verify that the firewall on each of your PCs has the proper IP address range added to the trusted zone.

- If you have enabled WEP or WPA encryption on your router, your wireless PCs will be able to connect only if the correct type of encryption is specified and if they have the correct key. Remember that passphrases are case sensitive. Also, if you enter the encryption key directly, the only acceptable characters are the numbers 0–9 and letters A–F.

# Summary

Just as you wouldn't leave your doors unlocked and your credit cards sitting around in the open, you don't want to leave your home network open to outside attack, either. In this chapter, you learned about some important steps you can take to secure your network. You saw that a firewall helps prevent intrusions and that you can make your wireless network a bit more private by properly configuring your router. You also learned that up-to-date antivirus software is a vital piece of your home network's security puzzle.

Now that you learned to secure your home network, the next chapter teaches you how to share it. Sharing is a vital link in making your network more useful.

# Things You'll Learn

- Why sharing is important
- How to share files, Internet connections, and printers
- Keeping your private files private
- Bringing in the neighbors

# Chapter 8

# Sharing Your Network

Now it is time to make your home network into something useful. The main reason for having a network is so that you can share things, which might include files such as digital images, a broadband Internet connection, or even a printer. A network is essentially useless if it isn't used for some type of sharing.

In this chapter, you learn how to safely share the resources of your home network. You'll see how to make files, connections, and printers available and how to restrict access when necessary.

 **NOTE**  As important as it is to share things on your home network, it's also important to realize that simply opening up everything for unlimited access isn't a reasonable solution. That's why it's vital that you read Chapter 7, "Making Your Network Secure: Locking the Network's Door," before you begin with this chapter. After you have read Chapter 7, you will understand how you can prevent outsiders from easily accessing your home network.

## Setting Up Shares: Getting to Files, Folders, and Printers on Your Network

If you have been in a rush to begin using your new home network, you might be frustrated to discover that it seems like the network simply isn't working. In this case, what seems to be true probably isn't. Your network probably is working properly, but you haven't completed the vital step of setting up *network shares*, and this is preventing you from making effective use of your network. Fortunately, setting up the shares is a simple task that will only take a few minutes to complete.

# Sharing Your Files

Sharing your files enables other users on your network to use those files. Generally speaking, what you are actually sharing is access to specific folders rather than to individual files. The access rights that you grant a user apply to all the files within that folder.

 **CAUTION**   Unless you specifically restrict access to specific subfolders, the access rights you grant to a parent folder apply to its entire tree of subfolders, too. That's why it's not a good idea to share your entire hard drive. Doing so would permit other people on your network to browse all your folders.

Different versions of Windows have slightly different sharing options available. For the most part, these differences aren't likely to be as important on your home network as they might be in an office setting. The following example assumes a home network setting; therefore, it doesn't cover more complicated issues such as assigning different people to user groups.

 **NOTE**   The Network dialog box in Windows 98 and Windows Me includes a File and Printer Sharing option that must be enabled using the Properties button to allow sharing. You open this dialog box by clicking the Network icon in the Control Panel.

**Step-by-Step: Sharing Folders on Your Home Network**

To share certain folders on your home network so that other users can access those folders, follow these steps:

**Step 1.** Open Windows Explorer. You might have a desktop shortcut you can click, or you might have to navigate the Start menu to do so. The exact location varies depending on your version of Windows.

**Step 2.** In the Windows Explorer folder tree (along the left side of the Windows Explorer window), right-click the folder that you want to share. This displays a popup menu, as shown in Figure 8-1.

**Figure 8-1** Find the Folder to Share in the Windows Explorer Window

Right-click the folder to share.

Select Sharing from the popup menu.

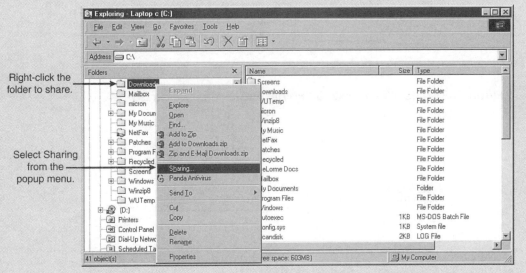

**Step 3.** Select **Sharing** to display the Sharing tab of the Properties dialog box for the selected folder.

Figure 8-2 shows how this dialog box appears in Windows 98 and Windows Me. Figure 8-3 shows this dialog box in Windows 2000. Windows XP displays a dialog box similar to the one in Windows 2000.

**Figure 8-2**   The Windows 98 Folder Properties Dialog Box

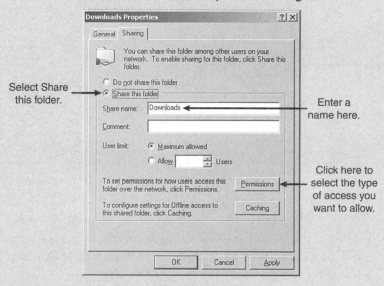

Select
Shared As.

Enter a
name here.

Select the type
of access you
want to allow.

Enter any
password
you want
to use.

Click OK to
continue.

**Figure 8-3**   The Windows 2000 Folder Properties Dialog Box

Select Share
this folder.

Enter a
name here.

Click here to
select the type
of access you
want to allow.

**Step 4.**   Select the **Shared As** (Windows 98 and Windows Me) or the **Share this folder** option (Windows 2000 and Windows XP).

**Step 5.** Enter a descriptive name in the Share name text box. The default name that Windows automatically places in this box might be acceptable, but you need to use a name that everyone can recognize easily.

**Step 6.** Select the type of access you want to grant by making a choice in the Access Type section (Windows 98 and Windows Me) of the dialog box or by clicking the **Permissions** button (Windows 2000 and Windows XP) and then making your choices.

There are several levels of permissions. Read-only allows someone to view files but not to create or modify them. Full allows complete access. Passwords or user groups can be used to further control access types.

**Step 7.** You might want to specify passwords for certain types of access, but doing so will probably have limited effectiveness on a home network because family members are likely to share passwords.

**Step 8.** Click **OK** to close the dialog box and confirm your changes.

To stop sharing a folder, simply repeat this procedure but select Not Shared in Step 4.

 **TIP**  Remember to set up shares on each PC that you want to appear on the network. If no shares are set up on a PC, no one will be able to access that computer from the network.

To access shared folders on your network after those shares have been set up, you can open the My Network Places (or Network Neighborhood, depending on your version of Windows) icon on your desktop and then navigate to the desired folder. Alternatively, you will find My Network Places (or Network Neighborhood) at the bottom of the folder tree in Windows Explorer.

Each home network is unique, but even so, you might find some of the following ideas useful in determining what to share on your network:

- You can extend the useful life of older PCs (Windows 98 or later) with limited hard drive space by providing users with storage on a networked PC that has a large hard drive.

- The family's digital photos would be excellent candidates for storing in a shared network folder.

- Storing each family member's important documents in a central location using subfolders for each person makes it a lot easier to do periodic backups that protect everyone's files from loss.

- If one PC is designated as the family media center and used to store all music files, everyone can access those shared files from her own PC without duplicating the files and wasting disk space.

## Sharing a Printer

Almost every computer user has the need to print things from time to time, but few home PC users really need to have a printer all the time. Depending on where you use your home PCs, you might not even have room for a printer by each system. Sharing a printer on your home network can make a lot of sense, and doing so certainly cuts down on both clutter and expense.

 **TIP**  With the giveaway prices on cheap inkjet printers, it might be tempting to simply give everyone her own printer, but it's actually more economical to buy a higher-quality printer and share it. Supplies like ink cartridges that are too small and dry out too quickly drive up the per-page printing costs of cheap inkjet printers so much that using these printers becomes far more expensive than if you bought a better printer in the first place.

There are two basic methods for sharing a printer on your home network:

■ Share a printer that is connected directly to one of the PCs on the network. This option doesn't require you to buy special equipment, but it does limit where the shared printer can be located because printer cables typically are no more than about 10 feet long.

■ Use a network printer server device like the Linksys WPS54GU2 Wireless-G PrintServer shown in Figure 8-4. This is a small box that connects to either your wired or wireless network and allows the printer to be placed in a central location that is convenient for the whole family.

You should choose the option that makes the most sense for your family.

**Figure 8-4**    The Linksys WPS54GU2 Wireless-G PrintServer Enables Printer Sharing on Your Home Network

The following step-by-step procedure shows you how to share a printer that is connected directly to one of your home PCs.

**Step-by-Step: Sharing Printers on Your Home Network**

To share printers that are connected directly to a PC on your home network, follow these steps:

**Step 1.**   Click the Windows **Start** button and choose **Settings > Printers** (Windows 98 or Windows Me) or choose **Printers and Faxes** (Windows 2000 and Windows XP) to display the Printers folder.

**Step 2.**   In the Printers folder, right-click the printer that you want to share and choose **Sharing** to display the Sharing tab of the Properties dialog box for your printer. The appearance of this dialog box will vary slightly depending on your version of Windows and on the make and model of your printer. Figure 8-5 shows this dialog box as it appears for an HP Color LaserJet 4550 in Windows XP.

**Figure 8-5**   The Sharing Tab of the Printer Properties Dialog Box

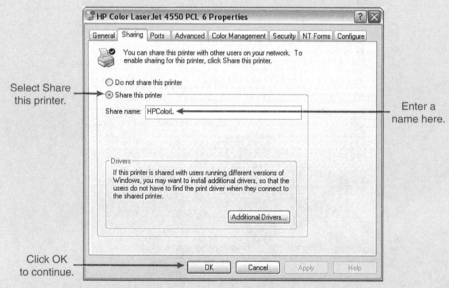

**Step 3.** Select the **Share this printer** option.

**Step 4.** Enter a descriptive name for the printer in the Share name text box.

**Step 5.** If the PCs on your home network are running different versions of Windows, click the **Additional Drivers** button (if it is displayed) to add drivers for those other Windows versions.

If the Additional Drivers button is not available, you can still add the printer to your other PCs using the Add Printer icon in each of their Printers folders, but you might need the driver disc for the printer to install the drivers on each PC individually.

**Step 6.** Click **OK** to close the dialog box and confirm your changes.

After you have shared the printer, it will be necessary to use the Add Printer icon in each PC's Printers folder to add that printer. Be sure to select the network printer option rather than the local printer option. (See Figure 8-6.) This will enable you to use the Add Printer Wizard to find the printer on your network.

**Figure 8-6**      Select Network Printer

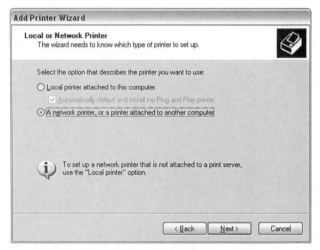

 **TIP**    Click the **Print Test Page** button in the Printer Properties dialog box to test the connection and ensure that the printer is set up properly.

# Sharing Your Broadband Connection

One of the easiest things to share on your home network is your broadband Internet connection. The reason for this is that your router automatically shares this connection, and there's no need for you to do additional network configuration to make this feature work.

You might have heard that Windows offers a feature called *Internet Connection Sharing (ICS)*. The ICS feature shares an Internet connection on a home network by having one PC connect directly to the Internet and also to the network. In effect, the ICS computer is taking the place of the router.

Even though ICS can work, it is far more difficult to set up and far more likely to cause connection problems for the other PCs on the network compared to simply using a router. In addition, if the ICS PC is shut down or if it crashes, everyone on the network will lose the Internet connection. To ensure a more reliable home network, use a router to share your Internet connection and avoid ICS. Of course, if a dialup Internet connection is your only option, ICS might be a serviceable choice.

## Sharing Over a Longer Distance

It might occur to you that sharing some of the resources of your home network over a longer distance than simply within your home would be possible. You might, for example, have a broadband Internet connection that you want to extend to your home office in your detached garage that's located at the back of your lot, or you might simply want to play networked games with a friend next door. Whatever the reason, wireless networking gear does make it possible for you to share your home network over a longer distance fairly easily. Yes, you can extend your network using a network cable, but wireless is easier because you don't have to string (or bury) a long cable.

 **CAUTION**  Internet service providers often frown upon the idea of neighbors sharing a broadband Internet connection. You should check the terms of the service agreement from your ISP before giving any thought to sharing your Internet connection. Violating the agreement could result in termination of your service or worse, and is definitely not recommended or advocated in this book.

Wireless networks use very high frequency radio waves to transmit data. These types of signals can travel over fairly long distances, but they're easily blocked by many different things. They don't go through metal, and thick masonry walls will also stop the signals. Even thick vegetation is enough to limit the range considerably.

Because the wireless networking signals are blocked so easily, you might not be able to rely upon being able to get the range or throughput that you want for your wireless network—especially if you place your router or access point on your desktop. Fortunately, you can do a number of things to improve the signal.

## Raising Your Router

The most obvious place to begin in attempting to improve your wireless network's signal range is to place your router (or access point) in a higher location. The top of a tall bookcase might be an excellent spot. You might also consider placing the router in your attic if you have one. The important thing to remember is to place it as high as possible and near the center of the area you want to cover.

There is one little problem with mounting your router in the highest possible location in your home—the router needs power, and you might not have a handy electrical outlet available. You could run a long extension cord, but doing so probably isn't going to make you very popular in the home décor department. Figure 8-7 shows a better solution. This is the Linksys WAPPOE Power Over Ethernet Adapter Kit. This kit uses some otherwise unused wires in the network cable that runs to the router to deliver power to the router.

**Figure 8-7**    Linksys WAPPOE Power Over Ethernet Adapter Kit

**NOTE**    The Linksys WAPPOE Power Over Ethernet Adapter Kit includes a special 48-volt power supply that must be used in place of your router's normal power supply. This higher voltage enables the kit to send power over longer network cables. The adapter that plugs into the network cable at the router end reduces the voltage to the proper level for your router. Be sure to save and label the router's original power supply in the event you might need it in the future.

## Raising Your Antenna

Depending on your situation, you might want to consider another method of getting your router's signal into a higher location. Rather than moving your router, it might be easier to simply move the router's antenna.

Because of the extremely high frequencies that are used for wireless networking, it's somewhat difficult to find the proper extension cables to allow you to reposition your router's antenna. Cables that are used for TV antennas, for example, simply won't work. You need a cable that is designed for the purpose like the Extenna shown in Figure 8-8. This cable uses special wire and connectors that are intended for the purpose. The Extenna is available in 3- and 7-foot lengths from http://www.extenna.com.

**Figure 8-8**    The Extenna Antenna Extension Cable

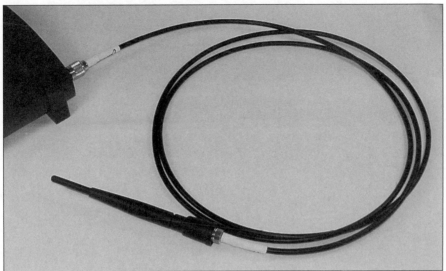

 **NOTE**   You must buy a cable that uses the correct connectors to fit the antenna on your router, access point, wireless bridge, or network adapter. Be sure to check the list of supported devices on the Extenna website before ordering. If you are unsure about which cable you need, ask for help by sending an e-mail to info@cantenna.com and include the exact model of the device you want to connect to.

## Adding an External Antenna

The standard (omnidirectional) antennas that come on wireless networking equipment radiate their signals in all directions. Normally, this is what you want, but it's not the best solution if you are trying to extend the range in a specific direction. For that purpose, a directional antenna is a better choice because a directional antenna concentrates the signal in a specific direction or arc. By concentrating the signal, you get a stronger signal over a longer distance.

Antennas boost signals to varying degrees as measured by a number called "dBi." The higher the dBi rating of the product, the further that antenna will reach.

One very interesting external antenna is the Super Cantenna shown in Figure 8-9. This unit can be mounted outdoors and offers a gain of 12 dBi—which will typically extend your signal to about four times the normal range of the standard antennas. You can find out more about the Super Cantenna at http://www.cantenna.com.

**Figure 8-9**     The Super Cantenna External Antenna

If you aren't trying to extend your wireless network between two different buildings but find that you can't get a good signal at the far end of your house, you might want to consider something like the 2.4-GHz Range Extender 6-dBi Desktop Directional antenna from Pacific Wireless, as shown in Figure 8-10. This handy little unit is easy to hide on top of a bookcase or even to mount flat on the wall, and it typically doubles the range compared to the standard antennas. You can find out more about this (and other external antenna options) at http://www.pacwireless.com.

**Figure 8-10** The Pacific Wireless Desktop Directional External Antenna

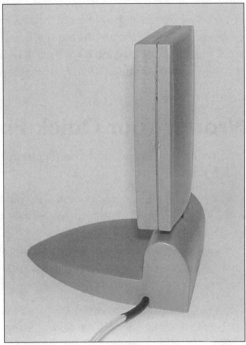

As with an antenna extension cable, it's important to buy an external antenna and connecting cable that matches the router or other equipment you are using.

 **TIP** All Linksys routers, access points, and wireless bridges have removable antennas so that you can use an external antenna. If the antenna won't unscrew easily, gently pull the boot at the base of the antenna away from the router or other device until you can unscrew the antenna.

Another option you might want to consider is to add a second access point in a different part of your home. You'll have to run a network cable to that second access point, of course. In addition, you'll need to set the second access point to use a different channel to avoid interference problems. It might also be necessary to use a different channel even if you only have one router or access point to avoid interference from a neighbor's wireless network.

## Limiting Remote Access: Keeping It Private

It's important to remember that by extending the range of your wireless network, you have also extended the distance at which strangers would be able to connect to your network. Be sure to review the security measures discussed in Chapter 7 to make certain that you've done everything possible to keep your extended wireless home network safe.

# What Went Wrong: Your Quick Fix Reference

Setting up your network for sharing is typically not too difficult, but if you have problems, here are some troubleshooting tips:

- If you have tried to extend your wireless network signal by pointing a directional antenna through a window, you might be frustrated to discover that the signals don't seem to go very far. There are a couple of possible reasons for this. A metal screen will stop the signal, but even a window without a screen will block the signal if the window is made using low-E glass—which most modern windows contain. Your only option might be to place the antenna outside.

- If your router won't power up when it is connected using a power over Ethernet kit, the problem could be an incorrectly wired network cable. In particular, a Cat3 cable typically doesn't have the extra wires needed to send the power for the router. Try a different, high-quality Cat5 or Cat5E cable.

- If you add an external antenna to a device that has two antennas, you might find that your results are somewhat unsatisfying because of interference between the two antennas. Use the advanced setup screens in the router's (or other device) configuration utility to set the router to use only the antenna connector that is attached to the external antenna. The default setting is always *diversity,* which uses both antennas. You will want to choose either right or left, depending on where you've connected the external antenna.

- Your PCs need to be in the same workgroup to share files on your home network. If you've set up network shares but still can't share files, see Chapter 6, "Configuring Your Network: Bringing Everything Together," for information on making sure that you have specified your workgroup properly.

- If you share a printer that is connected to a Windows XP or Windows 2000 system, you might have to use the Security tab of the printer's Properties dialog box to enable each user to access the printer. You can either use the Add button to add individual users, or you can simply make certain that the "Everyone" user has permission to print.

- Wireless network antennas must point in the same direction for the best signal. If you have some antennas oriented vertically and some horizontally, you'll probably have shorter range or might not be able to connect at all. Antenna orientation is especially critical with external directional antennas.

- If one of the PCs on your network is unable to connect to both the Internet and your network, check the IP address of that PC's network adapter as discussed in Chapter 5, "Installing Your Network Hardware: This Won't Hurt a Bit." Incorrect IP addresses can result from having drivers for more than one network adapter installed. Uninstalling unnecessary drivers might resolve the problem.

- Manufacturers sometimes upgrade the internal software (called *firmware*) in devices such as routers and network adapters. These upgrades often correct various newly discovered problems and might make it easier for you to make reliable connections. See the user manual for your devices to learn how to check for available firmware upgrades.

## Summary

In this chapter, you learned how to set up your home network to share files, printers, and your Internet connection. This chapter also discussed how to extend the range over which you share your wireless network by repositioning your router, moving its antenna to a different location, or using an external antenna.

The next chapter shows you how to make your home network an important part of your entertainment. You'll see that with the correct devices, your network can provide a lot of fun for the whole family.

# Things You'll Learn

- Creating a network entertainment center
- Adding your game console to the network
- Listening to Internet radio
- Using streaming media
- Setting up a webcam

# Chapter 9

# The Magic of Entertainment Options

Now that you have your home network set up and functioning, it's time to consider adding some additional items such as a media center, a game console, or even a webcam that will provide a lot of fun and entertainment. This is, after all, your *home* network, so there's no reason why it can't be used for quite different purposes than the typical office network.

The whole idea of using a network for entertainment is a relatively new one. As such, the options that are available to you are expanding almost daily. Consider this chapter to be just the tip of the iceberg, and you'll probably be pretty close to the truth, but at least you'll have an understanding of where to begin.

## Network Entertainment Centers: Spreading the Fun Around the House

One of the first entertainment options you might want to consider is setting up an unused (or underused) PC as a network entertainment center. Basically, this is simply a PC that you'll use as a central storage and distribution point for music, photos, video, and so on. Figure 9-1 gives you an idea of how this might look in your home.

**Figure 9-1**     Using a PC as a Network Entertainment Center

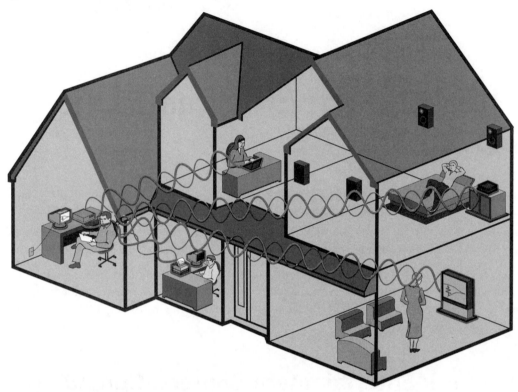

The PC you use as your network entertainment center has to be connected to your network wirelessly or via Ethernet, but it can be anywhere on the network at all—it doesn't have to be a particular place. This means that you can place this PC wherever you feel is the most convenient spot. Your other PCs will simply use the network to access the files on the network entertainment center.

The network entertainment center PC can be a PC that a family member uses for other purposes, but it's usually best to dedicate a PC for this single purpose if you can because doing so will reduce the hassles for the whole family. You don't need to have a monitor connected to this PC, and you might not need a keyboard or mouse, either. (Most PCs can boot without a mouse or keyboard—especially if they are running Windows 2000 or Windows XP.) But you're probably wondering how you'll control a PC without a keyboard, mouse, or monitor. The answer is to use a remote control program like TridiaVNC or TridiaVNC Pro (as shown in Figure 9-2).

**Figure 9-2** Using TridiaVNC Pro to Control the Network Entertainment Center PC

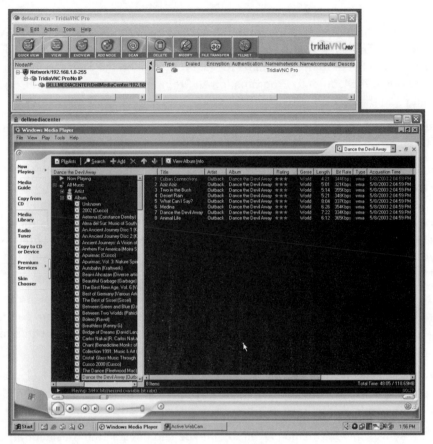

TridiaVNC is a free program that you can download from the Tridia website at http://www.tridiavnc.com. TridiaVNC Pro is not free, but you might want to compare the features of the Pro version with the free version to see which best suits your needs. You can use the Pro version free for 30 days if you'd like to give it a try.

**NOTE** If all the PCs on your home network are running Windows XP, you might prefer to use the built-in Remote Desktop Connection. Unfortunately, this option does not support any previous version of Windows, so if you have any PCs that are not running Windows XP, you won't be able to use the Remote Desktop Connection. Because an older PC that you set up as a network entertainment center will likely be using an older version of Windows, one of the free VNC versions might be a better choice. In addition to TridiaVNC, you might want to consider the version known as Real VNC from http://www.realvnc.com.

Here are some suggestions about how you can make a PC into your home network entertainment center:

- Set up your choice of media player (such as Windows Media Player, RealPlayer, or MusicMatch Jukebox) so that it automatically loads whenever Windows starts. Just add it to the Startup folder under Programs (or All Programs) on the Start menu. You can do so by dragging the icon onto Programs (or All Programs) on the Start menu, and then dropping it in the Startup folder.

- If you use remote control software such as TridiaVNC, make sure that you configure it to start automatically whenever Windows starts.

- Configure your media player to copy audio CDs automatically to the home network entertainment center's hard drive whenever a new CD is inserted and to automatically download album information from the Internet. In Windows Media Player, you select **Tools > Options** and select the **Copy CD when inserted** checkbox on the Copy Music tab of the Options dialog box to do so. Other media players offer similar options, but you might need to check the online help to determine the precise commands you need to use.

- Buy the necessary adapter cable to connect the line out jack on the home network entertainment center PC to an auxiliary input on your home stereo system so that you can play the music you've saved on the stereo. Typically, this is a cable with a mini-stereo plug at one end and red and white RCA plugs at the other end.

- If the PC you're using as a network entertainment center is more than a few years old, consider upgrading the audio card because this could greatly improve the sound quality. Or, it could enable you to use a PC that currently lacks audio capabilities.

- Set up play lists in your media player so that you can have all the music for an entire party programmed and ready to play before any guests arrive.

# Wireless Media Adapters: Connecting More Than PCs

As an alternative to connecting a PC directly to your stereo system, you might want to consider using something like the Linksys WMA11B Wireless B Media Adapter shown in Figure 9-3. This compact unit can deliver music or pictures from a PC on your network to your stereo or TV, and it connects to your network either wirelessly or via a wired connection.

**Figure 9-3**    The Linksys WMA11B Wireless B Media Adapter

The Linksys WMA11B Wireless B Media Adapter includes a remote control so that you can select music or pictures without the need to sit down at a keyboard. Using the WMA11B also frees you from the fuss with installing a media player, configuring the Windows startup menu, or worrying about PC booting problems.

 **NOTE**    One thing that the Linksys WMA11B Wireless B Media Adapter cannot do is play video content from your PC on your TV. Unfortunately, this is simply a limitation of the bandwidth that is available on wireless 802.11b networks. See the next section, "Streaming Media: Movies and Fun on Demand," for more information on this subject.

# Streaming Media:
# Movies and Fun on Demand

When you think of home entertainment, you probably think about something beyond still images and music. Video content such as TV shows and movies is what most people really want, and you can use your home network to provide that type of entertainment, too.

In recent years, devices like Tivo and ReplayTV have become quite popular. These devices are called *personal video recorders* (PVR) and are popular for a number of reasons including

- PVRs enable you to view TV shows when it's convenient for you.

- PVRs enable you to pause or even rewind live TV.

- PVRs enable you to instantly skip commercial breaks.

- PVRs typically offer an onscreen guide that allows you to easily choose the shows you want to watch or record.

If you like the idea of a PVR but don't like the idea of paying a subscription fee for the onscreen guides, you might want to consider a different option that uses your home network and your PCs. Beyond TV (see Figure 9-4) from SnapStream Media (http://www.snapstream.com) provides everything that a standalone PVR does plus a lot of things that no PVR is capable of doing. For example, Beyond TV enables you to stream either live or recorded TV shows to any PC on your home network—even to PCs that don't have a TV tuner installed. Beyond TV also includes a free onscreen program guide so you won't be stuck with paying for a guide every month, either.

Beyond TV works with a number of different PC TV tuners, and you can use it over the air, cable, or even satellite TV receivers. You'll even find a 21-day trial version available for download at the SnapStream Media website (along with full details about several different TV tuners you can buy if your home network doesn't already have a PC with a TV tuner).

 **TIP** If you're looking for movies to download and view on your home network, one good place to begin is the Movielink website at http://www.movielink.com.

In most cases, you'll probably watch any PC-based video content on your computer's monitor. If you want to watch on your big-screen TV, you'll need a PC that has a *TV out* connector on its video card. ATI (http://www.ati.com) offers several video cards with this feature, including some models in the All-In-Wonder line that also have built-in TV tuners. The TV out connector must also match one of the available inputs on your TV. It will either a yellow RCA jack or an S-Video jack.

**Figure 9-4**    Beyond TV Enables Every PC on Your Home Network to Display
Live or Recorded TV Shows

# Internet Radio: Music and News from Around the World

The Internet has certainly brought some interesting changes to the world, and one area where these changes are really becoming evident is Internet radio stations. If you would like to listen to news or music from around the world, Internet radio makes it possible. If you're bored with the selections that your local radio stations keep repeating, there's bound to be an Internet radio station that will be playing some fresh music you won't hear on your FM radio.

The Internet radio station selections include live streams from broadcast stations and stations that are exclusively Internet-based. You can listen to stations that are located anywhere in the world, because the Internet removes distance as a factor. Some streams work best with broadband connections, but many are available even if you have only a dialup connection.

**TIP** If you have a PC set up as a network entertainment center, you can play Internet radio stations through your home stereo system.

Most media player software offers a selection of Internet radio stations (but not all stations are available in every different media player because of stream format differences). The following example uses Windows Media Player, but the method of playing Internet radio stations will be similar in the other players, too.

## Step-by-Step: Playing Internet Radio

To select and play Internet radio stations in Windows Media Player, follow these steps:

**Step 1.** Open the Windows Media Player. You might have an icon on your desktop or on the Quick Launch toolbar, or you can select **Windows Media Player** from the Programs menu.

**Step 2.** Click the **Radio Tuner** button along the left side of the Windows Media Player window to display the list of available stations. This might take a bit of time to display if your connection is slow.

**Step 3.** Select your favorite genre to display a list of stations.

**Step 4.** You might need to click the **Find More Stations** link near the upper right of the window to see a more complete listing.

**Step 5.** Click the listing for a station you want to hear to see the available options.

**Step 6.** Choose **Play** (or **Visit Website** if the **Play** option is not available). This displays the Now Playing screen, as shown in Figure 9-5. You can use the playback controls along the bottom of the screen to control the playback.

**Figure 9-5**     Internet Radio Stations Bring the Whole World to Your Home Network

# Online Gaming: Go One-On-One with Your Game Console

If you have a game console such as the Microsoft Xbox, Sony PS2, or Nintendo GameCube, you probably already know that online gaming is very popular. Each of these game consoles offers the option to play games against other players using an Internet connection.

Online gaming typically requires a broadband connection, and the one that provides Internet access to your home network is an ideal option. But if you have a wireless home network, there's just one problem—none of the game consoles comes equipped to connect to a wireless network.

Figure 9-6 shows an excellent solution to this problem. The Linksys WGA54G Wireless G Game Adapter provides the wired connection that your game console needs.

**Figure 9-6**    The Linksys WGA54G Wireless G Game Adapter

The WGA54G game adapter is very simple to install and use. You need to connect it to a PC to specify if the connection will be to the Internet or directly to another game console, but there are no drivers to install, and no additional configuration is required.

**TIP**  You can use two WGA54G game adapters to quickly network two game consoles in different parts of your house.

# Wireless Internet Cameras: Your Own Webcam

Webcams have hundreds of uses. People use them to show the current view out their window, to check to see who is at the front door, to monitor the inhabitants of their fish tank, and to keep watch over their home while they're away—just to name a few of those uses. Whatever your reason for wanting a webcam, the Linksys WVC11B Wireless B Internet Video Camera shown in Figure 9-7 might just be the ticket for your home network.

**Figure 9-7**     The Linksys WVC11B Wireless B Internet Video Camera

**CAUTION**  The WVC11B camera is not designed for outdoor use. It must be protected from getting wet because the unit is not waterproof and will likely be destroyed if you mount it outdoors.

Setting up the WVC11B camera is a very simple process. You simply insert the setup disc into the PC connected to the camera and follow the prompts. However, you should consider several important points as you set up the camera:

- Unlike the setup utilities for other Linksys equipment, you must enter **admin** in both the name and password fields.

- You set up the camera using a wired connection even if you intend to use the camera on a wireless network.

- If you want to make the camera visible on the Internet, you will have to subscribe to the SoloLink DDNS Service using the SoloLink option on the main screen of the camera's setup wizard. This SoloLink option is a subscription-based service that provides a fixed IP address for your webcam. Keep in mind, though, that your Internet service provider (ISP) might place limits on the amount of data you can transfer, and a constant video stream might exceed your limits.

- You access most of the camera's options using your web browser. If you did not change the default IP address, you can find the camera at http://192.168.1.115. If you did change the default IP address, you'll have to use whatever address you specified.

Although setting up the basic options for the WVC11B camera is quite simple, it can be a little complicated finding and configuring the option to send a short video clip via e-mail whenever the camera detects motion. The following step-by-step procedure shows you how to configure the camera for this purpose.

**Step-by-Step: Setting Up Your Webcam as a Security Camera**

To set up the WVC11B camera so that it sends out a short video clip via e-mail whenever the camera detects motion, follow these steps:

**Step 1.** Open Internet Explorer. You might have an icon on your desktop or on the Quick Launch toolbar, or you can select **Internet Explorer** from the Programs menu.

**Step 2.** Enter the IP address for the camera in the address bar. If you did not change the default settings, this will be **192.168.1.115**.

**Step 3.** Click **Go** to display the camera's web-based utility.

**Step 4.** Click **Setup** in the menu.

**Step 5.** Enter **admin** in both the name and password boxes, and click **OK** to display the setup screen.

**Step 6.** Click **Advanced** to display the options shown in Figure 9-8.

**Step 7.** Select the **Send E-Mail Alert when Motion Detected** checkbox.

**Step 8.** Click **OK** to confirm the message warning that changes in light levels can trigger motion detection.

**Step 9.** Choose the desired sensitivity from the drop-down Motion Sensitivity list box. Higher settings will result in more e-mails from the camera because the camera will be triggered more easily. Be sure to test your setting to make certain it works as you expect.

**Step 10.** Choose the length of the video clip from the drop-down Length of e-mail Video list box.

**Step 11.** Choose the setting you prefer from the Minimum time between e-mails list box.

**Step 12.** Enter the correct information in the **Send to**, **Show "From" as**, **Subject**, and **Outgoing Mail SMTP Server** text boxes. The Outgoing Mail SMTP server is the same one you normally use to send e-mail messages.

**Figure 9-8**  Advanced Setup for WVC11B Camera

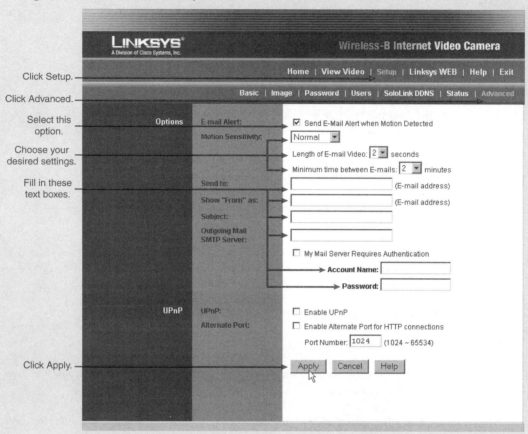

Click Setup.

Click Advanced.

Select this option.

Choose your desired settings.

Fill in these text boxes.

Click Apply.

**Step 13.** If your outgoing server requires authentication, select the **My Mail Server Requires Authentication** checkbox and enter the username and password values.

If you are unsure if your outgoing server requires authentication, check the account settings in your e-mail client software such as Outlook or Outlook Express. You will use the same settings as shown there.

**Step 14.** Click **Apply** to apply your changes.

Setting Up Your Webcam as a Security Camera

# Alternative Webcam Software

Although the webcam software that comes with the WVC11B camera is useful, it is somewhat limited. Figure 9-9 shows another alternative that you might want to consider—Active WebCam from Pysoft (http://www.pysoft.com). Active WebCam includes some important features such as the capability to send a new image to your website at specified intervals (to greatly reduce the amount of data you are transferring) and to automatically alternate between several cameras so that several different views can be displayed.

**Figure 9-9**   Active WebCam Supercharges Your Webcam with Additional Capabilities

# What Went Wrong: Your Quick Fix Reference

If you encounter problems with some of the home network add-ons mentioned in this chapter, here are some possible solutions:

- Some PCs will refuse to boot if a keyboard or mouse isn't present. If you are having trouble getting your network entertainment center PC to start, attach a monitor and watch the onscreen messages when you turn on the PC. If you see a message telling you that the system cannot start because the keyboard (or mouse) is missing, you'll need to have a keyboard (or mouse) attached. If you don't want the keyboard to be in the way, consider switching to a wireless keyboard. You might also want to consult your owner's manual to see if it has instructions on changing the Basic Input Output System (BIOS) configuration to allow booting without a keyboard and mouse.

- If your WMA11B Wireless B Media Adapter won't respond to the remote control, make certain that you are pointing the remote directly at the front of the media adapter. The remote control uses infrared light and will work only if it is pointed directly at the sensor near the top of the front of the unit. When installing the unit, make sure it is oriented so that the remote can reach the sensor.

- If you don't see the Radio Tuner button along the left side of the Windows Media Player window, the program might be in *skin mode*. Right-click on the Windows Media Player window and choose Switch to Full Mode from the popup menu to display the buttons.

- If the Internet radio station you're listening to repeatedly stops playing, you might need to choose a lower-bandwidth radio station. Look for the number shown in the Speed column of the radio tuner pane when you're choosing a station. Lower numbers indicate lower bandwidth (and lower sound quality). Look for the 28-kbps feeds if you're using a dialup connection.

- If you hear frequent clicks from the speakers while listening to Internet radio stations, close any Internet Explorer windows that might be open. Also, look for a link on the now-playing pane that says something like "Refresh on Demand" and click it to stop automatic downloads of new information because these downloads often cause clicks.

- When you move a WVC11B camera from a wired network connection to a wireless one, the IP address for the camera might change, making it somewhat difficult to find the camera on your network. Although the camera viewer utility can locate the correct IP address, you might want to use a fixed or "static" IP address when you set up the camera to avoid this problem.

# Summary

In this chapter, you learned about some of the really fun ways to use your home network for family entertainment. Of course, you can add many more things onto your network for even more enjoyment, but the sampling of options you saw here should at least get you thinking about how much your home network can increase your entertainment possibilities.

I hope you enjoyed learning how to choose and set up your own home network. I'm certain that your network will bring a lot of entertainment to your whole family, and I'm also certain that knowing how your network works will make it far easier for you to keep everything running smoothly.

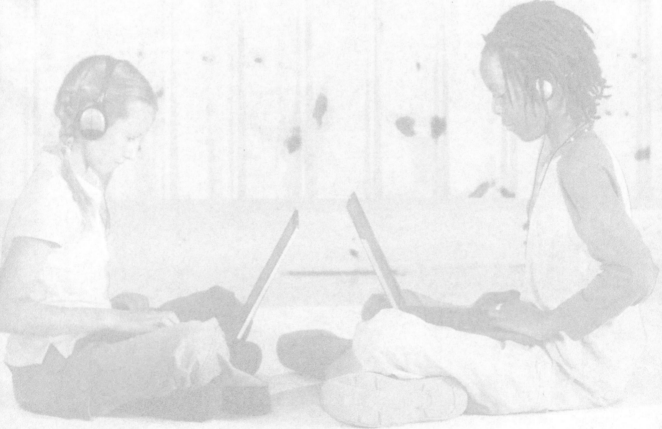

# Index

## Numerics

## A

## B

## C

# L

# M

# N

network interface cards (NICs). *See* NICs (network interface cards)

network protocols, 30

Network Setup Wizard (Windows XP), 87-96

networks, 6-8

  *see also* wired networks and wireless networks

  choosing, 35-38

  entertainment options, 14-19

  hardware

    *access points, 28*

    *gateways, 28*

    *hubs, 26*

    *network adapters, 25-26, 30*

    *routers, 27-28*

    *switches, 27*

  PC communication, 8-9

  sharing, 10

    *broadband connections, 150-156*

    *files, 10-12, 142-146*

    *folders, 142-146*

    *Internet connections, 12-14*

    *multimedia, 14*

    *printers, 12, 146-148, 150*

    *troubleshooting, 156-157*

  software, 29

    *drivers, 30*

    *network clients, 29*

    *protocols, 30*

NICs (network interface cards), 25

  drivers, 30

  installing, 67-83

  PC Card network adapters, installing, 82

  PCI network adapters, installing, 67-81

  USB network adapters, installing, 83

  wired networks, 54-56

Norton Internet Security, 113

  installing, 136-137

Norton Personal Firewall, 113

notebook computers, network adapters, 25

# O

office networks, home networks, compared, 8

omnidirectional antennas, 153

online games, 168

  firewalls, configuring for, 119-122

opening PCs, 67, 74-76

operating systems

  Windows 98, PC name setup, 99-101

  Windows 2000, PC name setup, 96-98

  Windows Me, PC name setup, 99-101

  Windows XP, home network configuration, 87-96

# P

Pacific Wireless Desktop Directional external antenna, 155

passwords, routers, setting, 122-125

PC Card network adapters, installing, 82

PCI network adapters, installing, 67-81

PCM100 EtherFast 10/100 Integrated PC cards, 39, 55

PCs (personal computers)

  configuring for home networks, 87-101

  naming

    *Windows 2000, 96-98*

    *Windows 98, 99-101*

    *Windows Me, 99-101*

  opening, 67, 74-76

performance, hardware, considerations, 49-50

personal video recorders (PVRs), 164

network clients, 29
protocols, 30
remote control programs, 160
webcams, 173
wireless networks, protocols, 42-44
**SpeedBooster, 57-58**
**SSID (service set identifier) broadcasts, changing, 126-128**
**streaming media, 164**
**subfolders, access, restricting, 142**
**Super Cantenna external antennas, 153-154**
**switches, 27**
Ethernet networks, 39
installing, 84
*troubleshooting, 85*
**Symantec, Norton Personal Firewall, 113**
**System Properties dialog box, 97**

# T

**TCP/IP (Transmission Control Protocol/Internet Protocol), 30**
**telephone networks, computer networks, compared, 6-7**
**threats (security), 111-112**
**Tivo, 164**
**traffic, controlling, firewalls, 113-119**
**Transmission Control Protocol/Internet Protocol (TCP/IP), 30**
**TridiaVNC Pro, 161**
**troubleshooting**
entertainment centers, 174
home network configurations, 106
network card installations, 85
network shares, 156-157
security, 138

# U

**USB cable, power line networks, 42**
**USB network adapters, installing, 83**
**USB200M EtherFast USB 2.0 10/100 Network Adapters, 39**

# V

**video cameras, 169-170**
alternative software, 173
as security cameras, 171-172
**video gaming (online), 168**
**viruses, preventing, antivirus software, 136-137**

# W

**WAPPOE Power Over Ethernet Adapter Kit, 151-152**
**WCG200 Wireless-G Cable Gateway, 52**
**webcams, 18, 169-170**
alternative software, 173
as security cameras, 171-172
**WEP (Wired Equivalent Privacy) encryption**
wireless networks, applying to, 133-136
WPA (Wi-Fi Equivalent Privacy) encryption, compared, 133
**WET54G Wireless-G Ethernet Bridges, 62**
**WGA54G Wireless-G Game Adapter, 16, 168**
**Wi-Fi networks.** *See* **wireless networks**
**Wi-Fi Protected Access (WPA) encryption, 133**
**Windows 98, PC names, setting up, 99-101**
**Windows 2000, PC names, setting up, 96-98**
**Windows Me, PC names, setting up, 99-101**

# Z

**ZoneAlarm, 113**
  configuring, 115-122
    *wireless networks, 122-136*
**ZoneAlarm Pro, 113**

**Cisco Press**

# NETWORK BUSINESS SERIES

## JUSTIFY YOUR NETWORK INVESTMENT

### Network Business books deliver:

**A clear and approachable writing style**—no in-depth technical knowledge required

**Technology overviews** that promote informed decision making

**Implementation scenarios** that outline various business models

**ROI and TCO metrics** that assist with complex technology decisions

**Interviews with industry leaders** that provide real-world insights on technology decisions

**Detailed case studies** that showcase relevant technologies

**Look for Network Business titles at your favorite bookseller**

**The Case for Virtual Business Processes**
Young / Jude • ISBN: 1-58720-087-2

**IP Telephony Unveiled**
Brown • ISBN: 1-58720-075-9

**Planet Broadband**
Yassini • ISBN: 1-58720-090-2

**Power Up Your Small-Medium Business**
Aber • ISBN: 1-58705-135-4

**The Road to IP Telephony**
Carhee • ISBN: 1-58720-088-0

**Taking Charge of Your VoIP Project**
Walker / Hicks • ISBN: 1-58720-092-9

**The Business Case for E-Learning**
Kelly / Nanjiani • ISBN: 1-58720-086-4 • Coming Soon

Network Business Series.    **Justify Your Network Investment.**

Visit **www.ciscopress.com/series** for details about the Network Business series and a complete list of titles.

**Cisco Press**

# FUNDAMENTALS SERIES
## ESSENTIAL EXPLANATIONS AND SOLUTIONS

When you need an authoritative introduction to a key networking topic, **reach for a Cisco Press Fundamentals book**. Learn about network topologies, deployment concepts, protocols, and management techniques and **master essential networking concepts and solutions**.

### Look for Fundamentals titles at your favorite bookseller

**802.11 Wireless LAN Fundamentals**
ISBN: 1-58705-077-3

**Cisco CallManager Fundamentals:**
**A Cisco AVVID Solution**
ISBN: 1-58705-008-0

**Data Center Fundamentals**
ISBN: 1-58705-023-4

**IP Addressing Fundamentals**
ISBN: 1-58705-067-6

**IP Routing Fundamentals**
ISBN: 1-57870-071-X

**Voice over IP Fundamentals**
ISBN: 1-57870-168-6

Visit **www.ciscopress.com/series** for details about the Fundamentals series and a complete list of titles.

Learning is serious business.
**Invest wisely.**

**Cisco Systems**

**Cisco Press**

# CISCO CERTIFICATION SELF-STUDY
## #1 BEST-SELLING TITLES FROM CCNA® TO CCIE®

## Look for Cisco Press Certification Self-Study resources at your favorite bookseller

Learn the test topics with **Self-Study Guides**

**CCNA Self-Study:**
Interconnecting Cisco Network Devices (ICND)
Second Edition

Cisco authorized self-study book for CCNA® 640-801 and ICND 640-811 foundation learning

ciscopress.com

Edited by:
Steve McQuerry, CCIE® No. 6108

Gain hands-on experience with **Practical Studies** books

**CCNA® Practical Studies**

Practice for CCNA exam #640-807 with hands-on networking lab scenarios

ciscopress.com

Gary Heap, CCIE®
Lynn Maynes, CCIE

Prepare for the exam with **Exam Certification Guides**

Includes
NetSim LE
network simulation

**CCNA® Self-Study**
**CCNA ICND**
Exam Certification Guide

The official self-study test preparation guide for the Cisco CCNA ICND exam 640-811

ciscopress.com

Wendell Odom, CCIE® No. 1624

Practice testing skills and build confidence with **Flash Cards and Exam Practice Packs**

**CCNA® Self-Study**
**CCNA Flash Cards**
and Exam Practice Pack
Second Edition

More than 1100 flash cards, practice questions, and quick reference sheets for the CCNA 640-801, INTRO 640-821, and ICND 640-811 exams

ciscopress.com

Eric Rivard
Jim Doherty

Visit **www.ciscopress.com/series** to learn more about the Certification Self-Study product family and associated series.

Learning is serious business.
**Invest wisely.**

# Cisco Press

## CCIE PROFESSIONAL DEVELOPMENT
### RESOURCES FROM EXPERTS IN THE FIELD

CCIE Professional Development books are the **ultimate resource for advanced networking professionals,** providing practical insights for effective network design, deployment, and management. **Expert perspectives, in-depth technology discussions, and real-world implementation advice** also make these titles essential for anyone preparing for a CCIE® exam.

## Look for CCIE Professional Development titles at your favorite bookseller

**Cisco BGP-4 Command and Configuration Handbook**
ISBN: 1-58705-017-X

**Cisco LAN Switching**
ISBN: 1-57870-094-9

**Cisco OSPF Command and Configuration Handbook**
ISBN: 1-58705-071-4

**Inside Cisco IOS Software Architecture**
ISBN: 1-57870-181-3

**Network Security Principles and Practices**
ISBN: 1-58705-025-0

**Routing TCP/IP,** Volume I
ISBN: 1-57870-041-8

**Routing TCP/IP,** Volume II
ISBN: 1-57870-089-2

**Troubleshooting IP Routing Protocols**
ISBN: 1-58705-019-6

**Troubleshooting Remote Access Networks**
ISBN: 1-58705-076-5

Visit **www.ciscopress.com/series** for details about the CCIE Professional Development series and a complete list of titles.

Learning is serious business.
**Invest wisely.**

# Cisco Press

## NETWORKING TECHNOLOGY GUIDES
### MASTER THE NETWORK

Turn to Networking Technology Guides whenever you need **in-depth knowledge of complex networking technologies.** Written by leading networking authorities, these guides offer theoretical and practical knowledge for **real-world networking applications and solutions.**

## Look for Networking Technology Guides at your favorite bookseller

**Cisco Access Control Security: AAA Administration Services**
ISBN: 1-58705-124-9

**Cisco CallManager Best Practices: A Cisco AVVID Solution**
ISBN: 1-58705-139-7

**Designing Network Security,** Second Edition
ISBN: 1-58705-117-6

**Network Security Architectures**
ISBN: 1-58705-115-X

**Optical Network Design and Implementation**
ISBN: 1-58705-105-2

**Top-Down Network Design,** Second Edition
ISBN: 1-58705-152-4

**Troubleshooting Virtual Private Networks**
ISBN: 1-58705-104-4

Visit **www.ciscopress.com/series** for details about Networking Technology Guides and a complete list of titles.

Learning is serious business.
**Invest wisely.**

# Cisco Press

Learning is serious business.

**Invest wisely.**

# DISCUSS

## NETWORKING PRODUCTS AND TECHNOLOGIES WITH CISCO EXPERTS AND NETWORKING PROFESSIONALS WORLDWIDE

VISIT NETWORKING PROFESSIONALS
A CISCO ONLINE COMMUNITY
WWW.CISCO.COM/GO/DISCUSS

CISCO SYSTEMS

THIS IS THE POWER OF THE NETWORK. now.

Copyright © 2004 Cisco Systems, Inc. All rights reserved. Cisco Systems is a registered trademark of Cisco Systems, Inc. and/or its affiliates in the U.S. and certain other countries.

# SEARCH THOUSANDS OF BOOKS FROM LEADING PUBLISHERS

Safari® Bookshelf is a searchable electronic reference library for IT professionals that features more than 2,000 titles from technical publishers, including Cisco Press.

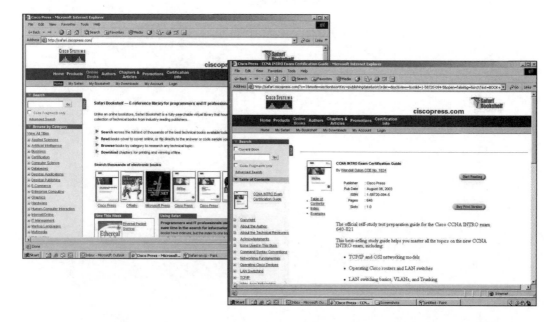

With Safari Bookshelf you can

- **Search** the full text of thousands of technical books, including more than 70 Cisco Press titles from authors such as Wendell Odom, Jeff Doyle, Bill Parkhurst, Sam Halabi, and Karl Solie.

- **Read** the books on My Bookshelf from cover to cover, or just flip to the information you need.

- **Browse** books by category to research any technical topic.

- **Download** chapters for printing and viewing offline.

With a customized library, you'll have access to your books when and where you need them—and all you need is a user name and password.

## TRY SAFARI BOOKSHELF FREE FOR 14 DAYS!

You can sign up to get a 10-slot Bookshelf free for the first 14 days.
Visit **http://safari.ciscopress.com** to register.

CISCO SYSTEMS

**Cisco Press**

# 3 STEPS TO LEARNING

**STEP 1**  **STEP 2**  **STEP 3**

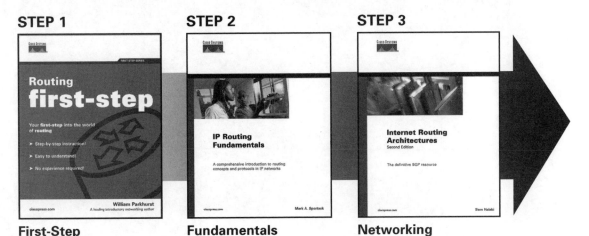

**First-Step**  **Fundamentals**  **Networking Technology Guides**

**STEP 1**  **First-Step**—Benefit from easy-to-grasp explanations. No experience required!

**STEP 2**  **Fundamentals**—Understand the purpose, application, and management of technology.

**STEP 3**  **Networking Technology Guides**—Gain the knowledge to master the challenge of the network.

## NETWORK BUSINESS SERIES

The Network Business series helps professionals tackle the business issues surrounding the network. Whether you are a seasoned IT professional or a business manager with minimal technical expertise, this series will help you understand the business case for technologies.

**Justify Your Network Investment.**

**Look for Cisco Press titles at your favorite bookseller today.**

Visit **www.ciscopress.com/series** for details on each of these book series.

Learning is serious business. **Invest wisely.**

# Cisco Press

# SAVE UP TO 25%

## Become a member and save at **ciscopress.com**!

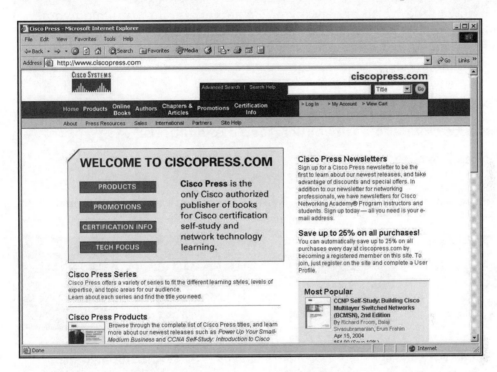

Complete a **User Profile** at ciscopress.com today to become a member and benefit from discounts of up to **25% on every purchase** at ciscopress.com, as well as a more customized user experience. You can also sign up to get your first **30 days FREE on InformIT Safari Bookshelf** and **preview Cisco Press content**. With Safari Bookshelf, you can access Cisco Press books online and build your own customized, searchable electronic reference library. And don't forget to subscribe to the monthly Cisco Press newsletter.

Visit **www.ciscopress.com/register** to sign up and start saving today!

The profile information we collect is used in aggregate to provide us with better insight into your technology interests and to create a better user experience for you. You must be logged into ciscopress.com to receive your discount. Discount is on Cisco Press products only; shipping and handling are not included.

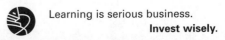

Learning is serious business.
**Invest wisely.**

CISCO SYSTEMS

**Cisco Press**

# Your first-step to networking starts here

Are you new to the world of networking? Whether you are beginning your networking career or simply need a better understanding of technology to gain more meaningful discussions with networking experts, Cisco Press First-Step books are right for you.

➤ **No experience required**

➤ **Includes clear and easily understood explanations**

➤ **Makes learning easy**

**Check out each of these First-Step books that cover key networking topics:**

- **Computer Networking First-Step** ISBN: 1-58720-101-1

- **LAN Switching First-Step** ISBN: 1-58720-100-3

- **Network Security First-Step** ISBN: 1-58720-099-6

- **Routing First-Step** ISBN: 1-58720-122-4

- **TCP/IP First-Step** ISBN: 1-58720-108-9

- **Wireless Networks First-Step** ISBN: 1-58720-111-9

Visit **www.ciscopress.com/firststep** to learn more.

## What's your next step?

Eager to dig deeper into networking technology? Cisco Press has the books that will help you move to the next level. Learn more at **www.ciscopress.com/series**.

**ciscopress.com**

**Learning begins with a first step.**